• THE SUN HISTORICAL SERIES •

ASSEMBLED FROM HARPER'S 1886, HARPER'S 1873, AND HARPER'S 1870

THE RIVER FROM THE VIADUCT.

Ohio 100 Years Ago

Compiled by Skip Whitson

SUN BOOKS

Sun Publishing Company
Albuquerque

First Printing — June 1977
Copyright © 1977 by Skip Whitson

SUN BOOKS
Are Published By
Sun Publishing Company
Post Office Box 4383
Albuquerque, New Mexico 87106
U.S.A.

SB-050
ISBN: 0-89540-050-2

Printed in the United States of America

List of Illustrations

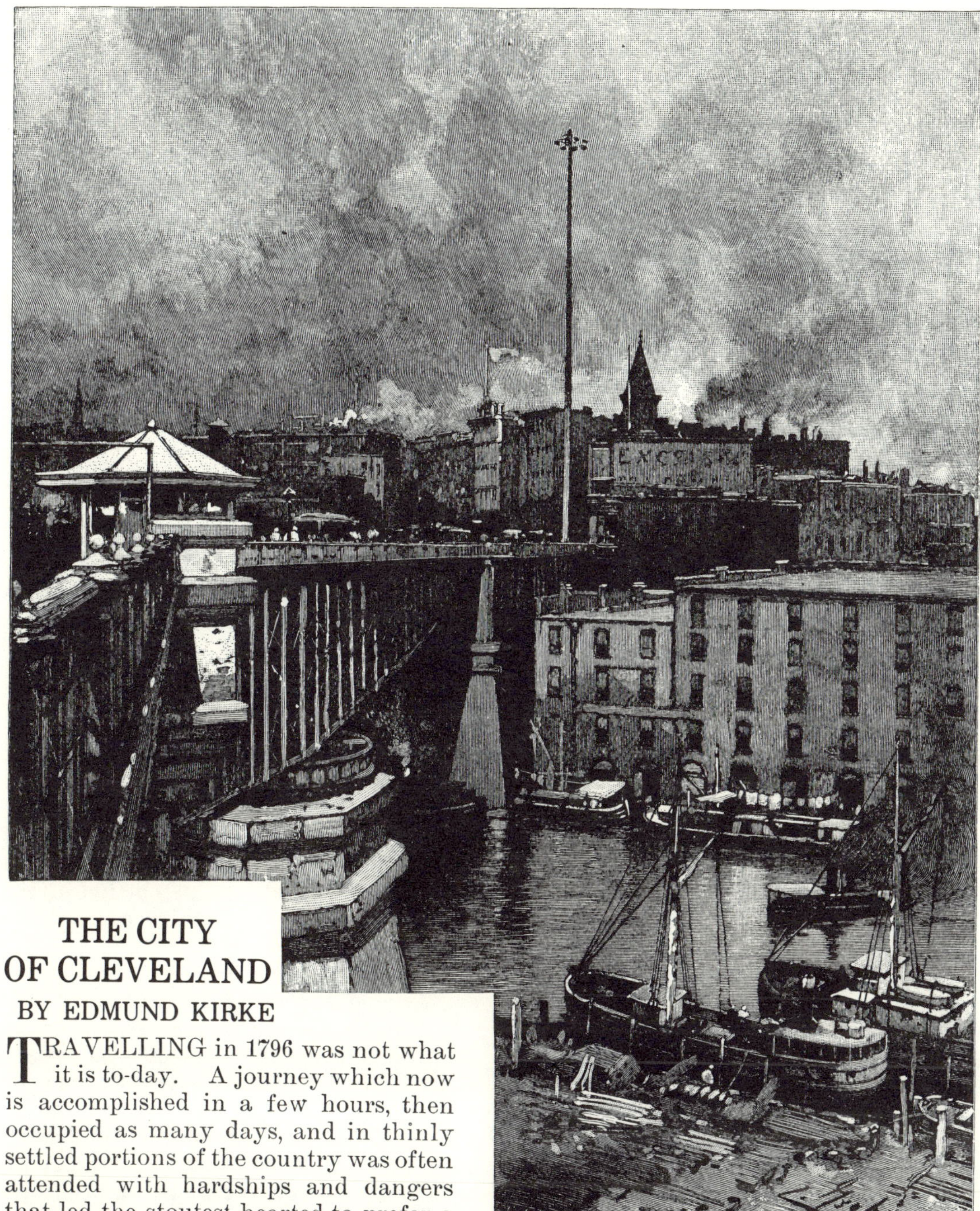

VIEW FROM THE VIADUCT.

THE CITY OF CLEVELAND

BY EDMUND KIRKE

TRAVELLING in 1796 was not what it is to-day. A journey which now is accomplished in a few hours, then occupied as many days, and in thinly settled portions of the country was often attended with hardships and dangers that led the stoutest-hearted to prefer a seat by their own firesides. This was, at least, the experience of a young New Hampshire farmer, who in the year I have mentioned set out to find for himself a home a thousand miles or more nearer to the setting sun. He was named James Kingsbury, and though born in Connecticut, had been reared among the granite hills, where the annual crop of stones is so large that the sheep's noses are said to be sharpened to enable them to nibble the thin grass that grows between them. He had heard of a country around the Great Lakes where the climate, being tempered by vast bodies of water, was mild and genial, and the soil so fertile that it only needed to be " tickled with a hoe to laugh into a harvest," and he determined to cast his lot in that delightful region.

The Revolution had left the country in poverty, and Kingsbury was no better off than the most of his neighbors, but though not yet thirty years of age, he had already attained to the rank of Colonel in the militia—a position which in those days implied character and a certain degree of social consideration. But he had a young family growing up around him, and it was probably more on their account than his own that he left the security of a settled district for the unknown hazards of a new country. Whatever may have been his motive, it is certain that in the early spring of 1796 he set out from Alstead, New Hampshire, with his wife and three children—the oldest not four years old—to find a home in what was then the far distant West.

He travelled by "private conveyance," taking with him a young brother of his wife to aid him on the journey. His outfit was a stout farm wagon drawn by a yoke of oxen, and laden with household goods and provisions; a horse to carry his wife and two younger children; a cow to supply milk during the journey; and for defense a rusty Queen's-arm musket, with which an older brother had in 1777 done effective service at Bennington. His first destination was Oswego, and after leaving Albany his route lay through a wild forest, where the road was merely a bridle-path blazed through the woods—the trail used from time immemorial by the Indians. Here no inn or friendly farm-house invited the traveller to lodge overnight, and the little company was forced to camp out among the trees, the woman and children sleeping in the wagon, while the man and the boy took turns in watching the fire, which had to be kept in a constant blaze to frighten away the wolves and panthers with which the forest was infested. Thirty days they journeyed in this manner, travelling perhaps ten miles in a day, before they came in sight of the little collection of log huts which then composed what is now the important port of Oswego.

Here Kingsbury found a scanty array of shipping, from among which he sought to find a craft suitable to navigate a lake subject at this season to violent storms, and at all times unsafe for any but skillful seamen. Nothing better presented itself than an open flat-bottomed boat, rigged with a single sail, and capable of carrying his family and household goods, but sure to have its gravity upset if freighted with animals ignorant of the science of equilibration. In this, however, Kingsbury embarked, closely hugging the land, and never venturing out in threatening weather,

the young lad meanwhile mounted upon his horse, and making his way through the woods along the shore with the cow and the oxen. At night the boat would be drawn up on the beach, and the camping-out experiences would be repeated. In this slow and toilsome way he journeyed another thirty days, when he arrived at Fort Niagara, which was the end of his route on Lake Ontario. Here the order of proceeding was reversed. The boat which had carried the wagon was now to be carried by that vehicle over the thirty miles of portage to Lake Erie. Here the little craft was again launched—trundled from the wagon into the lake—and here, at the future Buffalo, Kingsbury fell in with a gentleman who was to decide not only his destination, but his worldly destiny.

This was General Moses Cleveland—the Moses that was to lead a considerable part of Connecticut into the Ohio wilderness, and to come down to us as the founder of one of the most beautiful cities in the Union—Cleveland, Ohio. He was agent and director of the Connecticut Land Company, which had recently bought of that State the Western Reserve—a tract of about 3,500,000 acres, extending westward from Pennsylvania along the shore of Lake Erie, and "reserved" to Connecticut by the United States as its portion of the public domain. Cleveland was travelling in the wake of a surveying party of fifty, who had but recently gone forward to survey and lay out into townships and cities this immense tract, in readiness for the tide of emigration which was expected to follow. He had never seen his wide possessions, and they had never been explored; hence he could have given Kingsbury no reliable description of the country; but it is certain that he induced him to locate upon the reservation. In doing so, Kingsbury became the first white settler in northern Ohio.

Cleveland's first destination was Conneaut, a future village, near the junction of the lake and the line of Pennsylvania. Here Kingsbury selected a piece of ground on which the surveyors had already erected a cabin, and then broke up the soil and planted a few acres to serve his family for another season. During the winter that was approaching he expected to subsist on the provisions he had brought with him, eked out by what could be spared from the stores of the surveyors, whom he found at Conneaut, but who were soon to leave for a larger and more important town which was to be laid out at the westward. To the site of this town, which had been fixed upon by the company in Connecticut as the capital of the reservation, Cleveland made an ex-

a shore everywhere overhung by a dense green forest, which was beautifully mirrored in the waters below, and before many hours came upon a narrow opening between two low banks of sand. Pushing their canoes into this opening, they found a narrow channel, widening gradually to

MOSES CLEVELAND.

cursion with a small party soon after his arrival at Conneaut. The location had been determined on without any knowledge of the topography of the country, and merely because it was at the mouth of the Cuyahoga River.

The little party coasted closely along

the south, and bordered on the east by wooded bluffs, and on the west by broad flat marshes overgrown with reeds and coarse grass. Near the entrance the beach was a miry sponge, and they had to proceed some distance up the muddy stream before they could find a patch of solid ground large enough to sustain a landing. While they were doing this, the square-ly built, swarthy man who held the tiller of the leading boat had time to reflect upon the folly of locating a town without knowing something of the topography of the country. As the bow of his boat touched the land he sprang on shore, and clambering up the wooded slope at the east, looked off upon a broad level expanse ris-ing gently from the lake, and stretching away as far as his eye could reach to south-ward. At a glance he saw that this was the true site for his future city, and the low ground along the river merely the water gateway that should admit to it the vast commerce of the future. Of this future he had great expectations, but he did not live to see them realized. Dying within ten years, and while Cleveland was still a mere hamlet of log houses, he be-held its future greatness only from the Pisgah of a somewhat active imagination.

Leaving a few men to erect a store-house and cabin for the coming surveyors, Cleveland returned to Conneaut; and in the course of a short two months the city which is to bear his name to a late poster-ity came into existence—on paper. The map which was then made on the ground, by pasting together several sheets and parts of sheets of foolscap, was found a few years ago among the papers of ex-Governor Holley, of Connecticut, a son of one of the Cleveland surveyors. It is dated October 1, 1796; but the streets indi-cated upon it bear the same names and have the same locations as those now in existence.

Soon after the surveyors left Con-neaut, Kingsbury was called by important business to return to his former home in New Hampshire. It must have been ne-cessity which took him away, for he had to leave his wife and little ones, with only a lad of thirteen, exposed to the hazards of a wide forest frequented by roving bands of savages. Going on horseback by the shortest route—overland from Buf-falo to Albany—he expected to return by the 1st of December; but the time came without him, or any tidings of him, for no mails as yet travelled west of Fort Stanwix, near Utica. The winter set in early with great severity. Snow fell deep late in November, and well-nigh blockaded the lonely cabin, and soon the little fam-ily ran short of provisions, and the cattle of fodder. Till the snow came, the In-dians had brought the family game; but with the first very cold weather they had fled, with the birds, southward, and now the lone woman and her children seemed left to perish there in the heart of the wil-derness. To add to her trials, another child was then born into the household. But even then, thus sick and alone and shut out from all human succor, this heroic wo-man did not lose hope or courage, for she trusted in a Providence who hears even the cry of the ravens. She knew that, if alive, her husband would soon come to her rescue; but day after day she watched and waited for him, measuring carefully her scanty store of food, and listening with anxious ear to every sound that broke the stillness of the forest; but the days length-ened into weeks, and still he did not come.

She ministered to herself as well as she could, and at the end of a fortnight man-aged to drag herself about the cabin; and during this time another furious storm broke over the little cabin, lasting, with-out intermission, twenty-one days, and piling still higher the heavy drifts that everywhere covered the forest. Could her husband survive, exposed to such a frozen tempest? or if he did, was there hope he could reach her, buried as she was under drifts as high as the roof of her dwelling? Terrible and desolate was the outlook to the lonely woman; but her faith and trust and courage did not even then forsake her, and at last her patient waiting was rewarded. It was Christmas Eve when the storm cleared away, and a gleam of sunshine broke at last through the long overhanging clouds. She went to the window to watch the welcome light, and then she caught sight of her husband, struggling painfully through the heavy drifts on his way to the cabin. He was on foot, and only an Indian guide was with him. Slowly he came on, but at last he reached the house, and, scarcely able to speak, fell exhausted in the opened doorway.

The reason of his long delay was soon made known to the overjoyed woman. He had no sooner arrived at his old home than he was stricken down with a fever, the seeds of which he had carried from the malarial swamps of Conneaut. As soon as able to mount his horse he had set out to return; but the heavy snows in western New York had so impeded his progress that he did not reach Buffalo till the 3d of December. There, though scarce-

TRAVELLING IN THE OLDEN TIME.

ly able to sit his horse, he had halted only long enough to secure an Indian guide—for the snow had obliterated the trail, and none but a native could find the way through the forest in such weather. They had set out together on the following day; and thus he had been exposed, day and night, for three long weeks, to the storm that she had heard howl so furiously around the little cabin. The drifts in many places had been higher than his horse's head; in one of them the animal had perished, and he would have shared its fate but for the fidelity of the faithful Indian.

The rest of this "winter's tale" may be briefly related. The revulsion of feeling consequent on the return of her husband prostrated Mrs. Kingsbury. She was herself now attacked with the fever, and unable to give her child its natural nourishment. The life of the infant then hung upon that of the half-starved cow, whose sole subsistence was the small twigs of the linn, elm, and beech, which had been gathered for the winter's fodder. It was a fortnight before Kingsbury was enough recovered to move about, and then he had to face another journey. The stock of provisions had now become all but exhausted, and no supply could be obtained nearer than Erie, twenty-five miles distant. The intense cold which had succeeded the storm had thickly incrusted the snow, and over it, on foot and alone, he dragged a hand-sled laden with the precious eatables. Flour could not be procured, and only a bushel of wheat; but on this, cracked and boiled, they managed to keep their souls and bodies together.

But a great calamity soon befell the lonely household. Among the browse for the cattle, the young lad had gathered some twigs of the oak, not knowing that they were poison to dumb creatures. Of these the cow had eaten, and died; and thus the little child was doomed to starvation. Day after day, and night after night, the little thing wailed its life away, and that father and mother, powerless to help, were forced to listen. At last its wailing ceased; and then the man and the boy made for it a rude coffin from a pine box which had been left by the surveyors, and scooped for it a narrow bed amid the snow. Lifting it upon his shoulder, the father bore the little body from the house, and the mother lifted herself up in her bed to catch a last glimpse of it as he laid it away in a little mound not far from the dwelling. She watched him as he lowered it into the ground, and then she heard falling upon it the frozen sods that were to hide it from her eyes forever. With that sound she fell back unconscious, only to awake a fortnight later ignorant of all that had happened. Now the strange thing that we call life was in her only a flickering flame, which, if not quickly fed, would soon burn out in its socket. This the husband saw, and loading the old Queen's-arm, which is still a sacred relic in the family, he gathered up his little remaining strength and went out to secure some of the animal food that was necessary to the saving of his wife's life.

The severe weather had relaxed, and now, instead of cold blasts from the frozen lake, had come milder breezes from the south, bringing with them a few lonely birds into the forest. But the birds were shy, and Kingsbury would be fortunate to get within shooting distance. He trudged wearily on into the woods, but he saw no game, and at last, almost despondent, he sat down upon a fallen tree in the midst of a snow-bank. Soon a solitary pigeon came and perched itself upon the topmost branch of a tall tree at the utmost range of his musket. It seemed a hopeless chance; but he lifted his weapon and fired, and the bird fell, and he went home with it rejoicing. When he gave the broth to his wife she revived, and opening her eyes, asked, in a feeble tone, "James, where did you get this?" They were the first words she had spoken for a fortnight.

Such was the first winter of the first white settler in northern Ohio. It is not strange that, when the surveyors, coming to complete their work in the spring, told him that some of them intended to locate at the new city they had laid out at the westward, he should have decided to leave that desolate wilderness and build his cabin where he could occasionally see a human face of his own complexion. He did this, and thus became, in June, 1797, the first permanent settler in Cleveland, Ohio.

But he did not again make the mistake of locating near a marsh-bordered stream where the air was laden with malarial palsy. He moved back a mile and more from the Cuyahoga to a deserted cabin left by some Indian traders, who are supposed to have been there in 1786. This he occupied till he could build a cabin of his own, which he soon did, on a spot directly east of the public square, and not far from the present site of the Post-office. On the ground near by—now occupied by the City Hall and Catholic Cathedral—he planted a crop of corn, and thus provided against a repetition of the experiences of the previous winter.

Kingsbury's first neighbor, and the second settler at Cleveland, was one Lorenzo Carter, who soon afterward built a cabin at the mouth of the river, near the hut and store-house of the surveyors. These two families, in all nine persons, comprised the total population of Cleveland in 1797. In the following year four families were added to the settlement; but after that date the town increased very slowly, numbering in 1810 only fifty-seven persons, and as late as 1820 not more than

LORENZO CARTER.

one hundred and fifty. This snail-paced progress, due to a sterile soil and a malarial atmosphere, was, however, not shared by the adjacent country. More healthy and productive, this grew with amazing rapidity; and the consequence was that Cleveland, though small in itself, soon came to be of some importance as the mart and port of entry of a thriving farming region. This fact may justify a brief reference to the character, habits, and manner of life of its early settlers.

In 1800, Governor St. Clair appointed Kingsbury Judge of the Court of Common Pleas and Quarter Session of the county; and in the following year there came to reside in the place Samuel Huntington, a nephew of Governor Huntington, of Connecticut, and himself soon afterward Governor of Ohio. He was a man of cultivation, well descended, and eminent at the bar, and Kingsbury was a man highly esteemed; but in local influence they were both overshadowed by Lorenzo Carter, who had built his rough log cabin at the mouth of the river. This man was a genuine type of the pioneer. Though rude and uncultured, he was generous, kind-hearted, and neighborly.

He had a shrewd, active intellect, great physical strength, and a keen though crude sense of justice; and these qualities, combined with a somewhat aggressive and domineering temper, gave him great ascendency over the simple-minded settlers and rude aborigines. As early as 1798 a whiskey distillery had been put up by a man named Bryant near the mouth of the river, and the Indians flocked to it in crowds for supplies of fire-water. Carter's house was near by, the Indians met him, and he soon acquired an influence over them greater than that of their own chieftains. His word became law among them, and so it soon was with the white settlers. Where there is no regular administration of justice it is natural that the strongest should rule; but what was known as "Carter's law" had control in Cleveland long after a regularly organized court existed in the county. But the court sat at Warren, fifty miles away, and was not at first attended with such a degree of state as was calculated to impress very much awe upon the community. The first session is said to have been held in the open air, between two corn-cribs, Judge Kingsbury occupying a rude bench beneath a tree, the jurors sitting around on the grass, and the prisoners looking on from between the slats of the corn-cribs. On other occasions court was held in a barn, as being the most commodious building in the town.

Carter's law was administered with quite as little state, but it had the advantage of being more accessible and of much speedier execution. One or two instances will serve as illustrations. In 1807 a farm hand who had been working for a neighbor suddenly decamped, and his disappearance was reported to Carter as a strange thing, for he had stolen nothing, and had left behind some unpaid wages. "No man can leave this town in that manner," said Carter, at once mounting his horse and going after the runaway. Overtaking him, he bade the man return to the settlement; but he declined, protesting that he owed no one anything, and had a right to go and come as he pleased. Upon this, Carter poised his rifle, and gave the runaway his choice between returning peaceably, or being shot and left in the road, a prey to the turkey-buzzards. The man knew that Carter had a way of suiting his actions to his words, and he sensibly returned, received his wages, and continued a good citizen.

But Carter's law produced its most salutary effects among the Indians. On one occasion a large band of Ottawas and Chippewas had gathered on the west shore of the river, while a smaller gang of Senecas were encamped on the eastern bank, and in their mingling together a Seneca had killed an Ottawa. The deed was done at night-fall, and early on the following morning the combined Ottawas and Chippewas were seen arrayed in war-paint, and about to descend in vengeance upon the little band of Senecas. This being reported to Carter, he went among them, and by the promise of a gallon of whiskey, succeeded in compromising for the offense of the Seneca. Unfortunately the distillery was not in operation at the time, and the whiskey could not be delivered before the day following. But the Indians were impatient, and not disposed to wait the slow movements of the distiller. Again they put on their war-paint, and now they threatened extermination to both the whites and the Senecas. For a time it seemed as if nothing could appease their wrath, and that Cleveland was about to be sacrificed for the lack of a single gallon of corn whiskey. But, at the risk of his life, Carter went again among the infuriated savages, and again they took his word —this time, however, insisting upon two gallons of fire-water. Carter took good care that the distiller was not again tardy, and so the town, which had been kept awake by fear for a couple of nights, went again to peaceful slumbers.

Whiskey in the hands of Carter was a powerful persuader with the red man, as was shown on still another occasion. Cleveland had been made a county-seat in 1809, and this brought courts and justice nearer than fifty miles, and would be naturally expected to abolish Carter's law altogether. It did do this in a measure, but the sturdy pioneer had still so much influence as to be called upon in every sudden emergency. In 1812, an Indian was tried and condemned to death by the regular tribunal. Before being led to execution he boasted to Carter and others that he would show the white people how an Indian could die. He seemed to enjoy the ceremony of being drawn through the streets, to the sound of music, amid a crowd of people; but when he had ascended the scaffold, and the black cap was being drawn over his head, his fortitude forsook him, and he refused to be executed upon any consideration. In vain the sheriff appealed to his sense of manhood, and reminded him of his boast that he would die like a brave Indian. "Me will not die," was the only answer. Before resorting to unseemly force, the sheriff turned to Carter, who now ascended the scaffold, and said a few words to the Indian in his native language. Instantly the fellow wilted, and promised to die like a gentleman if Carter would give him just one-half pint of whiskey. The whiskey was sent for, but having imbibed it the Indian again refused to be executed. The sheriff was about to resort to force, but Carter suggested another glass of whiskey. The Indian accepted it, and then leaped fearlessly into eternity.

Whatever may be thought of his mode of conciliating the Indians, there is no question that Carter's popularity among them was a principal means of securing to the early settlers of Cleveland a freedom from savage molestation that was not enjoyed by other frontier settlements. There were among the early settlers men of greater cultivation and far higher character than Carter; but when he died, in

GOVERNOR HUNTINGTON ATTACKED BY WOLVES.

1814, he was universally regretted. Every one felt the community "could have better spared a better man."

More dreaded than the savages were the numerous wolves, bears, and panthers with which in those early days the woods were infested. They prowled about the highways, and often invaded the farm-yard of the settler. No one thought of going out at night unarmed, and though the dwelling-house was always unfastened—there being no fear of human intruders—a loaded musket hung constantly over the door as a defense from wild animals. As late as 1813 a large part of the town was covered with trees, and a forest of huge chestnuts skirted Superior Street, so dense as to completely shut the lake from the view of passers-by on the road. Near the corner of Euclid and Willson avenues was an extensive swamp, which was a favorite resort of wolves, and here, on one occasion, Governor Huntington was attacked by a pack of these hungry animals. He was mounted on a swift horse, and was returning from a circuit after dark, with no weapon but an umbrella, when in the midst of this swamp he was set upon by a score of these ferocious beasts. He laid about him right and left with his umbrella, and thus succeeded, not in beating off the attack, but in so frightening his horse that the latter outstripped the wolves and bore his rider off in safety.

But the panther was more dreaded than the wolf. He lurked everywhere about the wooded paths to spring upon the unwary traveller. Stretched along the overhanging branch of some tree, or concealed in the bushes by the way-side, he sought to take his prey unawares, and woe to the wayfarer who, after dark, had not both his eyes and his ears about him. In 1805, one of these creatures was killed in Euclid Avenue which measured nine feet from his nose to the tip of his tail. The bear, however, though less ferocious, was more troublesome than the panther. In broad daylight he entered dwellings and lapped up the housewife's cream, and at night he invaded barn-yards and pigsties, and made a feast of the calves and young porkers. If detected and pursued on such occasions, he would quietly walk off with a juvenile swine in his mouth, every now and then turning back and eying his pursuers with a cool impudence that defied everything but a well-loaded rifle. The passer to-day along Eu-

clid Avenue, who witnesses everywhere about him the evidences of culture, refinement, and the highest civilization, finds it hard to realize that within three-fourths of a century it has been a lair of wild beasts, when a steady arm and a trusty rifle were the settlers' only safeguards.

But we shall mistake if we suppose that in such a condition of things the settler's life was not one of comfort and enjoyment. When danger has grown familiar to us, it has lost half its terrors. Men are known to walk unconcerned into a powder mill with a lighted candle. The settler carried into the Western wilds the same free, elastic spirit he had known in his old home in New England. In fact, his life was the same, modified only by his primitive surroundings. But it was not the life of the rural New England of this generation. He wore no broadcloth, and she was not clad in silks, satins, and laces. His coat and trousers were of homespun gray, and she was arrayed in a cottonade gown, somewhat scant in the skirts, but hermetically sealed across the bosom, and adorned with an unaffected modesty that enchanted the beholder.

And this was their best apparel, in which they went to balls, attended meeting, and now and then listened to a Fourth of July oration, wherein the eagle expanded his wings and screamed in the most approved fashion. Balls were frequent, and to them the lads and lasses gathered from all the country round, mingling in the "mazy dance," and cutting the "pigeon-wing" to the tune of "Hi! Betty Martin," played by the old-fashioned fiddle, till the stars faded away in the morning. "Billing and cooing," it is said, filled up the intervals of the dance; but there being of that no positive testimony, it can not be stated as a historical fact. That interesting exercise is more likely to have occurred in some more secluded quarter—under green boughs, with an overhanging moon, or in the chimney-corner, while the old folks were snoring soundly in the adjoining apartment. That it did actually occur may, however, be safely affirmed, not only on good circumstantial evidence, but from the positive testimony of a white-haired veteran who not long ago related his own experience of those old days, at a gathering of the early settlers of this part of Ohio. The old gentleman gave so good a picture of those primitive times, which will never again be repeated in any section of this country, that I am tempted to transcribe a portion of his experiences.

Said the old gentleman: "The boys and girls who were predisposed to matrimony used to sit up together on Sunday nights, dressed in their Sunday clothes. They occupied usually a corner of the only family room of the cabin, while the bed of the old folks occupied the opposite corner, with blankets suspended around it for so as to produce a slight parental hacking cough. All this accords, in a great degree, with my own experience."

Then the ancient patriarch related his own courtship, told how he courted a girl of the "true Plymouth Rock stamp," who lived twenty miles away. As the course of true love never did run smooth, her mother objected to the match, and though he pleaded with her most pathetically, she

ROLLING-MILL.

curtains. About eight o'clock the younger children climbed the ladder in the corner, and went to bed in their bunks under the garret roof; and about an hour later father and mother retired behind the blanket-curtains, leaving the 'sparkers' sitting, at a respectful distance apart, before a capacious wood-fire-place, and looking thoughtfully into the cheerful flame, or perhaps into the future. The sparkers, however, soon broke the silence by stirring up the fire with a wooden shovel or poker, first one and then the other, and every time they resumed their seats, somehow the chairs manifested unusual attraction for closer contiguity. If chilly, the sparkers would sit close together to keep warm; if dark, to keep the bears off. Then came some whispering, with a hearty 'smack,' which broke the cabin stillness and disturbed the gentle breathing behind the suspended blankets, refused to melt "worth a cent." Then he went about for a time "sighing like a furnace," and then he sent his father to the court of the old lady to contract an alliance, offensive and defensive, but with no better success. He, however, kept on courting the girl till he loved everything on her father's farm, and at last his perseverance was rewarded, and the wedding day was fixed. The ague and fever was on him, and now, as the "day of days" approached, he often detected himself feeling his pulse, in fear that the disease might increase, and add to the fever already consuming him. But he was married without accident, and election soon coming off, he offered his vote at the polls. It was rejected because of his youthful appearance, and this his wife took much to heart. On the morning of the next election day she presented him with a small counterpart of himself. The news had preceded him at the polls, and his vote was not again questioned, though he was not yet of the legal age.

They were a stalwart race of men, and a glorious race of women. All of New England blood, they had the Yankee's adaptedness to circumstances, and his universal genius. The men could repair a plough, build a house, or drive a sharp bargain, and at the same time chop logic, discuss theology, or deliver a Fourth of July oration; while the women could brew and bake, turn a spinning-wheel, and make their children's clothes; or entertain guests, execute embroidery, or sing Watts's hymns in a way to set the birds a-listening. And all these things they did with equal ease, as if born to the vocation. What would be thought nowadays of a young maiden who, single-handed, should worst a bear in a deadly encounter, or who, in her father's absence, should shingle the roof and nail the clapboards upon his unfinished dwelling, and all the while be as much of a lady as any countess? But such were the Ohio girls of 1800 to 1820, and they were the mothers of the men who built the city of Cleveland—for the town was built by men, and not made by nature. Other places on the south shore of Lake Erie have as great natural advantages; but no other has had its men, and hence Cleveland has outstripped them all in commerce, wealth, and population.

In 1817 New York began the construction of the Erie Canal, and soon afterward Ohio conceived the idea of a similar work to connect Lake Erie with the Ohio River. Cleveland was then an insignificant village of about one hundred and fifty people; but its leading men had the foresight to see the advantage of making it the northern terminus of the great waterway, and they planned and worked to that end until it was accomplished. In 1827 the canal was completed as far as Akron, and this opened to Cleveland a rich farming section, already thickly settled and overflowing with surplus products. This surplus was brought to Cleveland, and merchandise was wanted in exchange; and thus sprang up a business which in a little more than one decade amounted to the annual sum of twenty million dollars. The lake commerce of Cleveland, which began in 1808 with Lorenzo Carter's sloop *Zephyr*, of thirty tons, now aggregates an annual tonnage of one and a half millions. In the second year after the opening of the canal it brought to the city 500,000 bushels of wheat, 100,000 barrels of flour, 1,000,000 pounds of butter, and of other produce a like proportion; and in the second year following (1830), the United States census found in the town 1075 people.

Among the earliest receipts by the canal was a boat-load of coal, for which an enterprising mine owner hoped to find a market in Cleveland. A wagon-load of it was hawked about the town, and attention called to its superior quality and great

ON THE RIVER.

THE RIVER FROM THE VIADUCT.

value as fuel. But the towns-people eyed it with disfavor. It was filthy, inconvenient to handle, emitted an offensive smoke, and not a few questioned if "stone" could be made to burn at all. With wood growing at their very doorways, what sense would there be in going a long distance for a fuel neither so clean nor so pleasant as the old-fashioned oak or hickory? All day long the wagon went the rounds without a single buyer; but after a time a good-natured innkeeper did consent to try a small quantity at two dollars per ton. This was the beginning of the coal trade of Cleveland, which now exceeds one million tons annually.

In 1832 the canal was finished to the Ohio River, and about the same time the advance-guard of that New England exodus which set in with the opening of the Erie Canal began to reach Cleveland and the outlying country. Its commerce grew with amazing rapidity. It numbered, in 1846, 10,135 people, and in 1852, 25,670; and this rapid growth was altogether due to the foresight of the man who conceived the idea of making it the northern terminus of the Ohio Canal. His name, I think, was Alfred Kelley, the first president of Cleveland village.

But about 1852 the commerce of Cleveland received a check, and its lake supremacy was threatened. The opening of through lines of railway had now begun to carry past its doors the produce on which its leading men had expected it to grow into a great commercial city. But these men were equal to the emergency. It occurred to them that the town was located about midway between the iron mines of Lake Superior and the coal fields of Ohio and Pennsylvania. They would bring the two together, and convert Cleveland into a great manufacturing city. This project resolved upon, they went about it with surprising energy. They erected foundries and factories, and set on foot a railroad down the Mahoning Valley, which should connect their furnaces with the immense coal fields of that region. This road was completed in 1857, and ever since the position of Cleveland has been assured as the great iron centre of the West. There is not here space to note the successive steps by which the place has since risen from a small town to a great city, but its progress is clearly indicated in the following figures from the United States census tables. In 1860 it had a population of 43,838; in 1870, 92,829; in 1880, 160,146; and by the best estimates it numbers at the present date upward of 200,000.

iron foundries and factories, oil and chemical works, brick-yards, and other manufactories impossible to enumerate. Here ten thousand machines move night and day in ceaseless hum, sending away, upon the numerous rail tracks which everywhere interlace the district, iron in its va-

CHARLES F. BROWNE ("ARTEMUS WARD").

If we stand on the precise spot where General Cleveland landed on that summer day in 1796, and look about us for a moment, we shall be able to form some idea of the great wealth and immense activity of this teeming hive of human industry. At our feet is an irregular valley, from a half to three-fourths of a mile wide, and following the windings of the river, which here doubles on itself several times, thus affording a long line of dock front within the city limits. The outer edges of this valley are flanked by high bluffs, on which are built the main portions of the town; but here, along the bed of the river, is the industrial heart of Cleveland. Looking up the valley, we see hundreds of acres, stretching from the lake shore to the southern boundary of the city, which are covered by ship and lumber yards, planing and flouring mills,

rious forms to the value of $70,000,000, and other products amounting to $30,000,000; that is to say, a total value of $100,000,000 yearly—an amount equal to the whole taxable property of the city. Six great lines of railway dip into this valley, bringing to it uncounted tons of raw material, and bearing from it, in thousands of cars, its immense manufactured product, ready for use and consumption. The spectacle is confusing. The frequent scream of the steam-whistle, the ceaseless whir of the heavy machinery, the constant coming and going of the loaded trains, with the harsh grating of their iron wheels, all this gets into one's head, till it turns around, and if he is a quiet man, and somewhat given to day-dreaming, he longs to be wafted back some three-fourths of a century to a seat at the hospitable board of Major Carter in the old log cabin that stood just yonder. If the old pioneer comes down here now, and has eyes to see what is going on about his old home, what must be his sensations!

Branching from this valley to the right is another valley skirting a narrow stream, which for a mile and a half is crowded with woollen factories, slaughter and packing houses, and similar establishments; and farther up the Cuyahoga, along the margin of another brook, is still another valley which pours a ceaseless tide of manufactured products into the immense commerce of Cleveland. This last stream is called Kingsbury Run, and it is the only memorial that I know of which has been dedicated to the worthy first settler.

Here, at the mouth of Kingsbury Run, are the works of the Standard Oil Company, covering several acres, and turning out, when in full operation, 10,000 barrels of oil daily. This concern is a marvel of commercial enterprise. Starting about the time that petroleum was discovered in Pennsylvania, as a private firm, with a capital of only $20,000, it has grown into a mammoth corporation having branches in half a dozen States, employing thousands of men, and handling nine-tenths of the oil product that goes to Europe. It is said to have bought out and frozen out a hundred rival establishments, to have made its own terms with railroads and yet enriched them by its traffic; and to now control the crude oil market of Pennsylvania, and the refined oil market of the world. Its blue barrels are to be seen all over Europe. It is stated that the profits of the company up to 1883 had been $77,105,322. Some of its business methods have been criticised; but however unscrupulous they may have been, the company is a wonderful exhibition of what business energy and sagacity may accomplish in this country.

Another gigantic business that has its home in this valley is that of the Cleveland Rolling-Mill, which owes its origin and wonderful success to the almost unaided efforts of the late Henry Chisholm, who came to America from Scotland, at the age of twenty, with scarcely a dollar in his pocket. By industry and energy he had, at the age of thirty-five, accumulated about twenty-five thousand dollars, and with this in 1857 he laid the foundation of this establishment, which is now one of the largest of its kind in the world, owning mines and mills in several of the States, and having, all told, a working force of 8000 men, 5000 of whom are employed in this valley. The rolling-mill has a capacity of 100,000 tons of steel rails per year, with four furnaces for the production of Bessemer metal. The aggregate business of the establishment amounts to $25,000,000 per annum.

Spanning this busy valley, and connecting the eastern and western halves of Cleveland, is a gigantic work, which has no parallel in any Western city. It is a stone causeway sixty-four feet wide, three-

LEONARD CASE.

fifths of a mile long, and carried over the Cuyahoga at a height of sixty-eight feet above the water. Its cost has exceeded two million dollars—an expenditure, in proportion to population, larger than that upon the Brooklyn Bridge.

If now we retrace our steps to the heart of the city, we shall see where the men live and transact their business who give life and movement to this busy hive of industry. Superior Street, the principal business thoroughfare, was laid out when land here was a drug in the market at one dollar an acre, and hence it is not surprising that the original surveyors made it a hundred and thirty-two feet wide. It is lined with stores, banks, and warehouses, some of which are business pal-

"I don't read anybody else," he answered, with a smile on his care-worn face; "he is inimitable." In the plain building before which we are standing the inimitable showman first set up his "wax figgers"; and if we enter here we may encounter the assistant editor of the *Plaindealer*, who was the associate and intimate friend of "A. Ward" when the latter was the city editor of this journal. He has many anecdotes to tell of the genial showman. He describes his appearance, when he first came

EUCLID AVENUE.

aces; but midway up the street we will pause for a moment before one of the least pretentious of these buildings.

Calling upon Mr. Lincoln on one of the darkest days in the late war, I was surprised to see upon his mantel-piece a couple of volumes—one a small Bible, the other, *Artemus Ward, his Book.* "Do you read Artemus Ward?" I asked him.

to the office, as decidedly rustic. He was, he says, long and lank, with flowing hair, and loosely fitting coat, and trousers too short in the legs and bagging at the knees. His humor was irrepressible, and always bubbling over, and he kept all about him in a constant state of merriment. He was a wag—nothing but a wag—but in that line a genius. He could see only the ludicrous side of a subject. Going away once on a short vacation, he engaged this

San Francisco to deliver a course in California. The season being close at hand, the manager asked him by telegraph: "What will you take for forty nights in California? Answer immediately." Ward answered immediately, by tele-

JOHN HAY.

gentleman to perform his work during his absence. He carefully instructed him as to his duties, and in doing so drew from his pocket a tow string about a foot and a half long, and told him he must furnish that amount of copy per day, leaving on his desk the measure as a reminder of the quantity. About this time he was called upon to respond to a toast to the Press at a Ben Franklin festival held in Cleveland. He rose to his feet, hung his head for a few moments in silence, and then sat down, having said nothing. In his account of the festival in the next day's *Plaindealer* his speech was reported by a blank space of about half a column of eloquent silence.

This gentleman remembers that soon after "A. Ward" entered the lecture field he was invited by a theatrical manager in

graph, "Brandy and water." The joke was noised throughout the State, and the result was, when Artemus went there to lecture on his own account, he was met everywhere with overflowing houses. While engaged in lecturing in the West, he wrote this gentleman the following epistle:

"MY DEAR GEORGE,—I want you to do me a favor. I relied on one of my men to save me the press notices. He didn't. Will you collect them for me at once, and send them to me at the Bates House? Now this is taxing your good-nature, but you'll do it for me—won't you, George? Do you know that you remind me more and more of the noble Romans? I don't know who they were, but you remind me of them; you do, indeed. And could I have appealed to one of those noble Romans to cut out some press notices for me in vain? I guess not. Go on, young man, go on. Deal kindly with the aged. Remember that we are here for only a little while, and that riches take unto themselves wings and fly away. Intoxicate the shunning bowl. Support your county paper. Love the Lord, and send me those notices. Write likewise. And now, kind sir, farewell. Farewell.

> "'When other lips and other hearts—'
> "Your'n, my pretty gazelle,
> "A. WARD."

Passing along Superior Street, we soon come to the public square laid out by the original surveyors. It is now called Monumental Park, from the fact that in one corner of it, on a high pedestal, stands a statue of Commodore Perry, in the attitude he is supposed to have occupied when about to charge upon the British squadron. The battle took place at Put-in-Bay, some miles to the westward, but it is said that the day before it was fought the fleet lay to off Cleveland, and was boarded by Judge Kingsbury, who had been engaged to furnish it supplies. Having told him that he was in hourly expectation of encountering the enemy, Perry added, "What would you do, judge, if he should heave in sight before you leave the ship?" "Do, sir?" answered the judge, already venerable for his gray hairs—"I would fight. I can do it as well as the best of you." The enemy did not heave in sight, and so the judge missed being one of the heroes of Lake Erie, and died peacefully in his bed at the great age of eighty.

It is said that the monument stands on the precise spot where Major Carter administered his last glass of whiskey to the refractory Indian, and where, too, in 1808, occurred the first sham fight and general training ever witnessed in Cleveland. The company numbered about fifty rank and file, and the men were arrayed in all sorts of costumes, and armed with all kinds of weapons, from a peeled club to a rusty musket. The captain wore a gaudy uniform, and a cocked hat surmounted by a rooster's tail. He gave his commands in a stentorian voice, and with a pompous stride in pace with the martial music. After putting his men through all sorts of evolutions, he bade them to charge upon the enemy. They did so. It was a whiskey barrel. And when the encounter was over, not one of them was able to tell whether he was dead or wounded.

The Park as originally laid out was a square plot of ten acres, but by the extension through it of two streets it has been divided into four smaller parks, one of which is occupied by the monument, another by a stone oratorium for Fourth of July and other orators, and the two others are ornamented with fountains and small lakes, tastefully fringed with flowers and flowering shrubs. It is in the heart of the business portion of the city, and near it are the Post-office and other buildings.

Before the present Post-office was erect-

A PICTURESQUE RESIDENCE.

ed, its site was occupied by a low wooden building, which was the meeting-place of perhaps the most unique club existing in this country. All may remember the story of "The First and Last Dinner," in which it is related how twelve friends of about the same age agreed one day, when met together at the Star and Garter Inn in Richmond, to institute an annual dinner among themselves, which each one should yearly attend until he was removed by death. The club should never admit any but the original members, and when one should die, his plate should be laid and his vacant chair be set at the table as if he were still with the remaining eleven. And this should go on, as one after another dropped out of his place, till the last one, the sole survivor of the twelve, should take his solitary seat in the silent room, and with the eleven empty plates and vacant chairs around him, should quaff his lonely glass of wine to the memory of his departed associates. This weird fancy of a fictitious story-teller has been rendered into actual fact in the intensely practical and prosaic city of Cleveland. Thirteen of the prominent citizens of the town met in 1836—nearly fifty years ago—in that old building, and formed a club, to include none but themselves, and to go out of existence with the life of the last member. There, in a quaint, old-fashioned room, furnished with a dozen or more chairs and a large round table, and ornamented with a few pictures, an old-fashioned fender and andirons, and a huge mantel, on which stood a couple of second-hand bottles doing duty as candlesticks, they came together week after week and year after year to play whist and chess, discuss important subjects, and talk over the news of the day. In 1858 all of them were living. The old building was christened "The Ark," and this name was transferred to the club, its members being called "Arkites." When the old house was demolished to make room for the Post-office, Mr. Leonard Case, one of the members, deeded rooms in Case Hall for the free use of the club till its last survivor should be no more. One of the members, an infirm, white-haired man of seventy-five, not long ago said to me, with a tremulous shake of the head, "We are all old men now; Mr. Case and five of the rest have gone, and very soon the last one of us will sit here alone."

From Monumental Park the leading streets ramify, not with the regularity of

RUINED TOWER IN WADE PARK.

the Detroit avenues, but in somewhat the same manner—branching off from a central hub like the spokes of a gigantic half-wheel, and spreading over the whole eastern part of the city. The most attractive of these streets is Euclid Avenue, which starts diagonally from the southwest corner of the square, runs to the city limits, and for many miles beyond through a most beautiful country. The portion nearer the Park is occupied generally for business purposes, and here are the Academy of Music, in which Clara Morris made her first appearance before the foot-lights, and other noticeable buildings. Beyond the business quarter the avenue is lined with private residences of such elegance as to well entitle it to its reputation of being the most beautiful street in the country. For a distance of fully three miles it is finely paved, level as a floor, and bordered by lawns of velvety softness. Each house stands at a distance from the street, and all have grounds more or less spacious, which are ornamented with shrubs and beds of flowers, and every here and there dotted with stately trees which stood there when the bear and the panther crouched amid their branches. No sameness wearies the eye, for there is everywhere variety both in the architecture and the treatment of the landscape.

surface, and is being developed with so much taste and judgment that it will eventually be the equal of any cemetery in the country.

Abreast of the business portion of the town, and on the shore of the lake, the city has recently converted a strip of waste ground into a most attractive park, which is also called Lake View. It was an unsightly bluff, seamed with gullies, and covered with wretched shanties; but the city took it in hand, planted trees, piled up rock-work, converted springs into fountains, and ragged gullies into beautiful ponds, and now it is one of the most at-

LAKE IN THE CEMETERY.

for there is everywhere variety both in the architecture and the treatment of the landscape.

Beyond these republican palaces is an exquisite private park, on which large sums of money and great skill in landscape gardening have been expended. It occupies a deep ravine and the adjoining uplands, and is threaded by walks and drives under wide-spreading trees, or amid a dense shrubbery whose fragrance perfumes all the air. The public-spirited projector of this park, Mr. J. H. Wade, the well-known electrician, is to convey it to the city as soon as a few preliminary conditions are fulfilled by the municipality.

Opposite this park, and overlooking the lake, is Lake View Cemetery, where Garfield's body is laid, and where the monument is to be erected to his memory. It occupies a tract of rather more than three hundred acres of beautifully diversified

tractive spots of the kind to be found anywhere. Every pleasant evening it is crowded with people who come here to inhale the cool breeze from the lake, and to watch the white sails and smoking steamers as they come and go on the blue water.

Of the western portion of the city, on the opposite side of the Cuyahoga, I can speak but briefly. The part nearest the river was originally the farm of Lorenzo Carter, and by his son was in 1830 sold to a company of speculators, who laid it out in streets, and here built what was called Ohio City. In 1854 it was annexed to Cleveland, and it now contains 60,000 inhabitants. Here is located a new city park, and the distributing reservoir of the Water Department. This is fed by a tunnel five feet in vertical diameter, which, sunk ninety feet below the surface, runs a mile and a quarter into the

LAKE VIEW PARK.

lake to obtain water free from the impurities which are brought down by the river. The capacity of the reservoir is six million gallons, and the total length of pipe laid, one hundred miles. The entire cost of works and pipe, from the crib in, has been nearly two million dollars.

As was to be expected of pilgrims from Connecticut, the first thought of the first settlers was for churches and schools for themselves and their children. Accordingly we find that as early as 1800 they invited here from their native State the Rev. Joseph Badger, a Congregational missionary, who went about among them, and preached in the open air or in the settlers' houses; and that two years later, Anna Spofford, the daughter of one of the first comers, gathered the little ones of the township into the "parlor" of Major Carter's log cabin, and taught their young ideas how to shoot in the right direction. This open-air church has grown into one hundred and fifty sacred edifices, some of them of the highest architectural beauty; and that one improvised school, into scores of educational palaces, where gather 50,000 children. And not content with providing the best system of instruction for the children, the people of Cleveland have organized an "Educational Bureau," managed by the first citizens, with the purpose to afford instruction and entertainment to the adult working classes by concerts, lectures, and gratuitous distribution of small books on useful subjects. Ten public entertainments have been given each season for three winters, the average attendance at which has been four thousand. The total distribution of books and pamphlets during the three years has been 167,200, and the average cost to each member, of each concert, lecture, and pamphlet, has been only three cents. The system is a most admira-

THE GARFIELD MONUMENT.

SCHOOL OF APPLIED SCIENCE.

ble one, and it deserves to be copied in other cities. The School of Applied Science is another of Cleveland's educational features.

Growing naturally out of the many churches of Cleveland are a host of benevolent institutions — hospitals, orphan asylums, retreats for the aged, children's homes, and Friendly Inns, in which latter the poor may find free reading-rooms, with the best of papers, magazines, and books; and also good meals and comfortable lodgings at a cost of merely enough to pay the expenses of the establishment.

Cleveland can not be called a literary centre, its men being of the class not of writers, but of workers; and yet it has been the home of several authors who have achieved distinction. Beside Artemus Ward, of whom I have spoken, it was at one time the residence of William Dean Howells, the most popular among living American novelists. Constance Fenimore Woolson, the author of "Anne" and "East Angels," was born in New Hampshire, but Cleveland has been the home of her girlhood and early womanhood. Here too resides John Hay, the widely known author of "Little Breeches" and "Castilian Days."

As every man is different in form, feature, and character from every other man, so in all these respects every town is different from every other town. In the youth of towns this individuality is more marked and observable than when, in their older years, foreign elements have blended with the native, and they have become more cosmopolitan. But even then, down at the root, in the inner spirit, the native

THE CRIB.

element controls, and gives its peculiar characteristics to the engrafted branches. So it is with Cleveland. A large foreign element has blended with the native, and somewhat modified its surface character, but the prominent features are still Yankee, and Connecticut Yankee at that. As Connecticut was sown with culled grain from Massachusetts, so northern Ohio was sown with culled grain from Connecticut, and this seed has produced a crop the like of which can be found nowhere else in this country. None of the first settlers are now living, but hundreds still linger on the Western Reserve whose memories go back to the time when Cleveland was an inconsiderable hamlet of not more than twenty houses. Some of these old worthies I have met, and one needs to meet them to realize what kind of men sprang from the loins of the New England of the year 1800.

Such a race accounts fully for the present generation which has builded Cleveland. If one were asked what is the prominent characteristic of these men of to-day, I think he would have to say, A large-minded and large-hearted liberality that does not stop to count any expenditure which may result in public good or benefit Cleveland. Scores of living men might be mentioned who would justify this remark. I may not speak of them; they are too many; but I may refer to two or three who are not living. One of these was Leonard Case, whose benefactions were simply princely; another was the late Henry Chisholm, whose benevolence flowed in a constant but unobtrusive stream, and who cared for the interests and studied the improvement of his army of 8000 workmen as if they had all been his own children; another was Joseph Perkins, who has recently died, mourned by the whole community; and still another was Amasa Stone, who while living gave half a million to Western Reserve College, and in dying left immense sums to educational and charitable institutions. And such men are still left in Cleveland. Now and then they are to be found in other cities, but here they are numerous enough to give character and tone to the whole community. With such men, and with its population increasing, its manufactures growing, and its trade expanding year by year in an almost unprecedented manner, it is not hazardous to predict that Cleveland will number five hundred thousand people by the close of this century.

OTHER TITLES IN THE *"OLD/100 YEARS AGO"* SERIES:

THE WINE ISLANDS OF LAKE ERIE

BY CONSTANCE F. WOOLSON

GATHERING THE GRAPES.

chords of music placed her, knowing what he did,

" where the lilies blow
Round an island there below,
The island of Shalott."

" Isles of the blest !" sighed the ancients, as they looked out over the unknown ocean, seeing in the hazy clouds of the horizon the purple shores of everlasting rest. And who among us, when traveling sad and weary over the waters, has not fallen into silence at the sight of far blue islands, mingling the Psalmist's wish, "O that I had wings like a dove ! for then would I fly away and be at rest," with dreams of the star islands in the sea of infinite space, whither we may be going after death, and where our loved ones may even now be awaiting us.

Erie is a dull lake, like persons one meets in life, neither beautiful nor ugly, neither strong nor weak, neither good nor bad. Its name signifies cat, given, say the first explorers, on account of the number of wild-cats upon its borders ; and as if this was not evil enough, the antiquated geography of Jedediah Morse, first published in 1789, describes the western end of the lake and its islands as so infested with rattlesnakes as to render it dangerous to land, acres of these creatures having been seen basking on the

TO the imagination there is something attractive in the very name of island. Robinson Crusoe on the main-land would lose the crown of his glory ; it is the island, the island, that fills the boyish heart with wondering interest. For children of a larger growth Reade takes up the tale, and his hero and heroine—but ordinary mortals in London—are invested with a strange romance when thrown together upon an island ; young love reads, young love dreams, and young love wishes,

" for thee and me,
A lone sweet isle amid the sea."

The representative Lady, type of the many isolated hearts who give their love to some unattainable ideal, lived upon an island ; the Master whose exquisite words are like

MEMORIAL TO COMMODORE PERRY, GIBRALTAR ISLAND.

lily leaves which stretched in every direction over the shallow water. At the present day the cats and rattlesnakes—unless, indeed, we except Reade's and Holmes's personifications of them—are gone; but the dullness remains, and we may sail from Buffalo to Cleveland, and from Cleveland to Detroit, we may cross and follow the Canada shore back again, and in all the 600 miles see nothing worth seeing save the man-made towns, so that we almost wish the eighteen thousand years which the Boston savants have assigned for the lake's evaporation might dwindle to eighteen, and thus let the Ohio corn fields spread their green ranks across to the Dominion shore. For from end to end there is no beauty in it. A Scotchman was once rallied about the total want of beauty in his betrothed. "Eh, lads," he answered, "dinna ye ken the dimple in her elbow?" And in like manner homely Erie has a dimple in her elbow, the group of islands in her southwest corner, as indistinct in the minds of most salt-water Americans as the Atlantis of the ancients. These islands, ten or more in number, varying in size from 2800 acres to a mere dot in the water, lie off Sandusky Bay, stretching out into the lake to meet their five Canadian sisters and the long point of Pelée. The large steamers on their way up and down the lakes pass north of these islands, and generally make the passage in the night, and thus in order to see them one must go to Sandusky, and sail out over its bay in one of the little steamers belonging to the island fleet—for these islanders are a maritime people, and own a small flotilla of all kinds of craft, from a steamer to a sloop for a one-man crew. Fishing boats, too, they have, in which they sail out to their fish-pounds, and come racing home wing-and-wing, loaded down with live fish crowded into their boat tanks. Then comes a lively scene, as the slippery creatures are thrown up into boxes standing on the dock, and so deftly is this managed that although tossed up with scarcely a glance, each squirming fish goes safely into his box, and is there transported into the interior, to be eaten by the farmers and their families; for here, as every where else, imported luxuries are preferred; the fish of the islands go into the interior, and the flesh of the interior goes out to the islands. The fish-pounds are numerous, and at night, when, as the law requires, they are all lighted up, the water looks as though a fairy fleet was sailing over it, so low down and so bright twinkle the little lights. Indeed, to a steady-going main-lander who does nothing by chance, the island fishery is but witching work at best. He has, perhaps, spent St. Martin's summer among the vineyards, eating the grapes and drinking the fresh juice from the presses, which, as the old English verse says,

"Saint Martin afterward
Alloweth to be wine—"

a most fortunate miracle for the health of the incautious drinker. But now he sees a cloud rising behind the purple mist; the Indian summer is over, and thoughts of the home fireside send him on board of the little steamer, which presently sails away, as he supposes, for Sandusky and the railroad. Mistaken supposition! The little boat circles round in the archipelago, now going one way and now another, now slowing, now hastening on, now turning her head inshore, and then suddenly backing out without stopping, until the bewildered traveler wonders whether a will-o'-the-wisp is at the bow. At length the charm is pointed out; it proves to be nothing more or less than a white rag. This sign, hung out on the end of a pole, means "fish," and as the catch is variable, and the stations numerous, the erratic course of the boat is explained.

It is within the memory of the generation now passing away that the Lake Erie islands came into the jurisdiction of civilization by means of a United States survey. Before that period their exact situation and size were unknown, and their few inhabitants were wild lords of the isles, beyond the reach of the law, who came occasionally to the main-land settlements to traffic away their rafts of cedar logs, but who lived generally by hunting and fishing, with just a suspicion of a taste for wrecking when the September gales threw a harvest along their shores. But when the Kelley family regularly purchased the island since called by their name, the largest of the American group, the day of squatter sovereignty was over, and the hybrid population, with its mud floors and

SHORES OF PUT-IN-BAY.—THE LAKE ERIE YACHT.

no windows, slowly gave place to settlers of a better class—slowly, since even now some of the islets are uninhabited, several have only a solitary family, and one, of course, has the traditional hermit who will not allow a woman's foot to touch the sacred soil of his retreat. The Indian names of the islands are gone, and they now bear the haphazard titles given to them by the sailors and settlers along shore: "Ballast," "Gibraltar," "Sugar," "Rattlesnake and the Rattles," "Green," "The Three Sisters," "The Three Bass," "Old Hen and Chickens," "Mouse," "Starve," "Pelée," and "Kelley's," the last formerly known as "Cunningham's."

The group has its page in history, a page which might well cause envy in the rich main-land cities cherishing a taste for historical societies, and burning for heroes to honor. Upon this page men well known in American annals appear, for the little archipelago has witnessed skirmishes and battles, plots and victories, in the past and in the present, for present still seems the war of the rebellion, although when we reckon them, nearly a decade of years has passed since its close.

First come the Indians. The story of the red men since the coming of Columbus is but a dreary series of wars and rumors of wars, broken truces, migrations, and never-ending trouble. Every plan has been tried, from gifts to rifle-balls, and every religious denomination has had an opportunity to try its moral suasion, while the impatient frontier soldiers and pioneers, who look upon Indians as so many wolves, have been held back by the strong arm of the law from the work of extermination. And what has been accomplished? Nothing. The few feeble successes gained at the expense of precious lives and heavy contributions of money can not color the mass any more than one drop can color a fountain. The Indian question has become a weariness to the nation, and there is a universal skipping whenever the popular heading of "Lo" appears in the newspaper column. With the universal habit of mortals, however, we cherish an interest in what is beyond our reach. Let an Indian tribe vanish entirely from the earth without leaving a shadow behind, not even one chieftain to go as a deputation to Washington, not even one brave who refuses to live upon his reservation, and skulks around the settlements clad in the cast-off silk hats of the white man, and forthwith we begin to exalt the extinct race with the heart of an antiquarian and the pen of a novelist. It is only the degenerate, mind-fatiguing Indians of to-day whom we despise; no doubt the tribes of the past were of a nobler nature. Among these tribes of the past there are none more completely past than the Eries, who have left scarcely more than a name behind them. They belonged to that remarkable confederacy of tribes called the Neutral Nation, dwelling upon the southern shore of Lake Erie, a city of refuge for warring parties on either side. To them belonged the right of lighting the council-fire of peace, a ceremony which was said to require a maiden hand, and for years they held their place, respected and at peace. Upon these western islands were some of their fastnesses; traces of their fortifications were discovered there by the first surveyors, earth-works built, apparently to inclose a village, with gates and sally-ports of wood, and in one place a quantity of new stone axes and arrow-heads stored away in a rude armory for future use. Picture-writing was also found, and one rock inscription upon Kelley's Island has been pronounced "the most extensive well-sculptured and well-preserved inscription ever found in America." The Eries were at the head of the Neutral Nation, and at the time of the first French explorers they were in the height of their power. So much is known, but no more. The Iroquois came and swept them from the face of the earth. "Of course," says the student of lake-country history, wearily. "The Iroquois are as sure to come sweeping in at the last as Sir William Johnson!" The Eries were so utterly destroyed that the most patient investigator can only say, "They were, and they are not." "Little besides their existence is known of them," says Parkman, whose histories are as reliable as they are fascinating—an unusual combination. It is an evil, no doubt, to be unreliable, but oh, is it not equally evil to be a Dry-as-dust?

A century and a half passed, during which the history of the lake islands is involved in obscurity, and then upon the scene steps Tecumseh, who belongs to Ohio and Lake Erie, as Pontiac belongs to the lovely Detroit River. The chieftain is near his end when we see him; he is making his last speech on the shore of the lake near the islands where he has watched the smoke of the battle at Put-in-Bay, and although he suspects the defeat of his allies, he scorns to retreat, and covers the British general with Indian satire. Standing upon the beach, and waving his hand toward the islands, in the name of all the tribes he speaks: "Father, listen! Our fleet has gone out; we know they have fought, we have heard the great guns, but we know not what has happened to our father with one arm" (alluding to Commodore Barclay, Perry's antagonist, who had lost an arm at Trafalgar). "Our ships have gone one way, and we are much astonished to see our father tying up every thing and preparing to run the other! You always told us you would never draw your foot off British ground, but now we see you drawing back without even a sight of the enemy, and we must compare our father's conduct to a fat dog who, when he is frightened, drops his tail and runs away! Father, listen! The Americans have not yet defeated us by land, and whether or not they have defeated us by water, we still wish to remain here and fight when they appear. You have the arms and ammunition which our great English father sent to his red children;

give them to us, and you may go, and welcome. But as for us, we are determined to stay, and, if the Great Spirit wills it so, we will leave our bones upon the land of our forefathers." For scathing rebuke and inflexible courage this red man's speech is admirable; and it was emphasized by his death in the first battle that ensued—a battle which he knew was hopeless before it began, but which his single determination absolutely held in the balance until death struck him down. As the historian says, "When his well-known voice was heard no more, the battle ceased."

The shade of the Indian has passed, and now enters the young commodore, who, upon the wild shores of Lake Erie, built a fleet from the trees of the forest, and almost nothing besides—a feat which in the mind of a modern ship-builder surpasses even the subsequent victory. With these vessels the young officer sailed up the lake to the islands, and there, off Put-in-Bay, he fought the battle of Lake Erie, September 10, 1813, the British fleet surrendering before sunset, and thereby giving up the whole lake to American control. The story of this battle has been told again and again, in prose and verse, in marble and oil. There is something in the motto which Perry hoisted just before the engagement which touches the popular fancy. "Don't give up the ship!" has become one of the people's sayings, and the dispatch announcing the victory, "We have met the enemy, and they are ours," has been adopted into the military language of the day; only Grant's "We will fight it out on this line, if it takes all summer," can compare with it. A deep principle often underlies a popular saying, as a deep feeling often underlies a popular song. Armies have ridden to victory on the chorus of a song, parties have carried a candidate into the White House on the wave of a saying. The class to which belongs George Eliot's Mr. Casaubon may, indeed, scorn any thing popular, but what are we all but people, and what is the world but the people's home!

After the battle the slain officers were buried on the shore of one of the islands: a willow-tree marks the spot. A remarkable incident, showing the power of sound, belongs to the story of the battle. A Cleveland pioneer was engaged that day in building the first log court-house on the public square, when suddenly he was startled by a sound which he supposed was thunder. There was not a cloud in the sky, however, and the wondering inhabitants gathered on the bank of the lake, thirty or forty in all, and looked toward the west, whence the strange sounds came. At length they recognized the report of cannon, and knowing that Perry's fleet had gone up toward the islands, they began to realize that a battle was taking place, and after a time actually distinguished the Amer-

THE STEAMER " MICHIGAN."—BURIAL-PLACE OF THE SLAIN IN THE BATTLE OF LAKE ERIE.

ican guns from the British, as the former were of heavier calibre. When, late in the afternoon, three loud reports were heard, evidently American, the listening band gave three hearty cheers, as sure of the unseen victory as though they had witnessed it from the shore of Put-in-Bay. The distance was seventy miles.

The next figures on the page of island history are the "patriots" of the Canadian movement for liberty in 1838. Sandusky was one of their points of rendezvous, and the islands were tempting strongholds; near Pelée Island they fought a battle with a force of British cavalry upon the ice, a novel battle-ground.

And now we come down to our own day, and face a figure not ten years dead—Beall, the pirate of Lake Erie. This young Virginian, an officer of the Confederate army, was hung as pirate and spy on Governor's Island, New York Harbor, February 24, 1865. The sentence was just, and its execution a necessary part of the discipline of war. Yet now that years have elapsed, and we can review the past without that terrible personal interest that made our hearts burn within us, there is something worthy of note in the story of this man, who, young, wealthy, and educated, threw himself, as it were, into the jaws of death from sincere though mistaken love for his native country.

John Yates Beall was a native of Jefferson County, Virginia. He graduated at the University of Virginia, Charlottesville, and at the breaking out of the rebellion owned a large plantation in his native county; his property was estimated at $1,500,000, and in addition he was said to be the heir of an estate in England. In the earliest days of the war Beall organized Company G, Second Virginia Infantry, and his regiment afterward formed part of the original "Stonewall Brigade," under Stonewall Jackson. He took part in many battles, but it is his piratical expedition among the islands of Lake Erie which brings him within the range of our subject—an expedition which ended in disaster and death. It is well remembered along the lake shore; Buffalo, Detroit, and Cleveland were filled with excitement; the citizens patrolled the streets by night, and visions of piratical craft sailing boldly in and firing upon the defenseless houses filled all eyes. Exhausted Ohio had sent into the field regiment after regiment beyond her quota, but her northern frontier was entirely exposed, and it seemed an easy thing to sail across from Canada and batter down her towns. Looking back upon it now, it still seems easy; and yet it was never done, although Canada swarmed with conspirators, under the leadership of Jacob Thompson, secret agent of the Confederate government. The United States had but one war vessel on the lakes, the *Michigan*, a paddle-wheel steamer, carrying eighteen guns. The capture of this boat would enable a small body of men to carry destruction from one end of the lake to the other. In September, 1864, the *Michigan* was lying off Johnson's Island, Sandusky Bay, which had been used since 1862 as a dépôt for prisoners of war; here were confined 2480 men, all, with the exception of about one hundred, officers of the Confederacy, enough to command an army of 80,000 men. The little island was naturally uppermost in the thoughts of the rebel officers in Canada. It was near at hand, a steamer could run across in the night, and in the winter a land force could attack it, for the ice was strong, and nowhere was there more than five miles between island and island, stretching like stepping-stones across the lake from Point Pelée to the Ohio main-land. No other prison was on an exposed frontier like this, and were it not for the guns of the *Michigan* a rescue might be effected: the *Michigan*, therefore, must be captured.

On the morning of the 19th of September the steamer *Philo Parsons*, plying between Detroit, the islands, and Sandusky, left Detroit at the usual hour on her way down the river; at Sandwich, on the Canadian side, four men came on board, and at Malden a party of twenty more, bringing with them a large old-fashioned trunk tied with ropes. As at this period there was a constant stream of fugitives crossing the border, fleeing from the draft, or coming back with empty pockets, this Malden party excited no comment, and the steamer went on her way through Lake Erie, stopping at the different islands, and taking on a number of passengers for Sandusky. After leaving Kelley's Island, the last of the group, suddenly four men came toward the clerk, who, owing to the absence of the captain, had command of the boat, and leveled revolvers at his head; at the same moment the old black trunk was opened, and the whole party armed themselves with navy revolvers, bowie-knives, and hatchets, and took possession of the defenseless boat. The course was then changed, and after cruising about at random for some time the pirates turned back to one of the islands—Middle Bass—and stopped at the dock. While here the *Island Queen*, a steamer plying between Sandusky and the islands, came alongside, and, suspecting nothing, threw out a plank in order to land some freight. Instantly the pirates swarmed up her sides, calling upon the captain to surrender; shots were fired—apparently more for the purpose of intimidation than for any real injury—knives and hatchets were held over the passengers, among whom were thirty or forty one-hundred-days' men on their way to Toledo to be mustered out. The pirates were few in number, but they were well armed, and held both steamers at their mercy. The captain of the *Island Queen* made sturdy resistance, endeavoring in vain to cut the ropes that bound his boat to the *Parsons;* and the engineer, refusing to obey the orders of the pirates, was shot in the cheek. Resistance was evidently useless; the passengers were put into the hold, with a guard over them, and the captain was asked if many strangers had come to Sandusky that morning, and if there was any excitement there. After some delay and discussion among themselves the pirates decided to exact an oath of secrecy for twenty-four hours from the women and citizen passengers, and allow them to go on shore, together with the hundred-days' men, whom they paroled, and then the two steamers, lashed together, started out toward Sandusky, the captain of the *Island Queen* being retained, with the hope that he could be forced to act as pilot. When four or five miles out the *Island Queen* was scuttled and abandoned, and the *Parsons* went on alone. A debate sprung up among the pirates as to whether or not they should run into Sandusky Bay; evidently something had failed them, some one had disappointed them. At length the captain was again put into the hold, the boat's speed was slackened, and she was kept cruising up and down outside as if waiting for a signal.

Chief in command of these raiders was John Yates Beall: his appearance and manner rendered him conspicuous among the others, who are described, in the language of one who saw them, as a "mean, low-lived set; Burley, the second in command, being a perfect desperado." In the report of Jacob Thompson, secret agent of the Confederacy in Canada, a document belonging to the rebel archives, the whole plot is related. There were two parts, the first being the expedition by water under Beall, and the second a conspiracy on shore, by means of which the officers of the *Michigan* were to be thrown off their guard, so that upon a given signal Beall could steam rapidly in, surprise them, and capture the boat. A cannon-shot sent over Johnson's Island was to tell the prisoners that the hour of rescue had come; Sandusky was next to be attacked, and after horses had been secured the prisoners were to mount and make for Cleveland, the boats co-operating, and from Cleveland strike across Ohio for Wheeling and the Virginia border. The key to the whole movement was the capture of the *Michigan*.

The plot on shore was headed by a Confederate officer named Cole. As has been related, Beall performed his part with entire success; and had the other head possessed equal capacity, no doubt the plan would have been successful, and the whole North taken by surprise at this daring raid and rescue upon a hitherto peaceful and unnoticed border. The two thousand young officers riding for their lives through the heart of Ohio, where there was no organized force to oppose them, would have seemed like a phantom band to the astonished inhabitants. Even the famous raid of John Morgan, well remembered in the great red-brick farm-houses of the central counties, would have been eclipsed by this flying troupe, the flower of the Southern army. On the lake Beall would have held the whole coast at his mercy, and the familiar old *Michigan*, turned into a piratical craft, would have carried terror into every harbor.

But the plot on shore failed. Cole spent his money freely in Sandusky, and managed to procure an introduction to the officers of the *Michigan*, inviting them to supper-parties, and playing the part of a genial host whose wines are good and generously offered. The tedium of the daily life upon the steamer and in the small town was enlivened by his hospitality, and for some time all went well; but gradually he began to mar his own plot by so much incautiousness and such a want of dexterity in his movements that a suspicion was aroused in Sandusky, and his manœuvres were watched. On the evening of the 19th of September Cole had invited the officers of the *Michigan* to a supper-party. Every thing was prepared for them, the wine was drugged, and when by this means they had been rendered helpless, a signal was to notify Beall that all was ready for his attack. But in the mean time suspicion had grown into certainty, and at the very moment of success Cole was arrested by order of the commander of the *Michigan*, the signal was never given, and Beall, on board of the *Parsons*, strained his eyes in vain toward San-dusky and Johnson's Island, cruising up and down outside the bay, now talking with his prisoner, the captain, and now urging his men to dare all and make the attack alone. But the men, a disorderly rabble gathered together in Canada, refused to enter the bay; and at last, disappointed and disheartened, Beall gave the signal to turn the boat, and abandoned the attempt. Back went the *Parsons*, with her pirate crew, past Kelley's Island, where the alarmed inhabitants were burying their valuables, and looking for the flames of burning Sandusky; past Middle Bass, where the unfortunate passengers, watching on the beach shortly after midnight, saw her fly by, the fire pouring out of her smoke-stacks, and "making for the Detroit River like a scared pickerel." The captain and those of the crew who had been retained to manage the boat were put ashore upon an uninhabited island, and after reaching the Canadian shore and scuttling the steamer, the pirates disbanded, and Beall, the master-spirit, was left to brood over a failure which had the additional bitterness of possible success.

In the morning the lake-country people woke up to hear the news. Incendiaries and conspirators in their midst, raiders by land and pirates by sea—these were the tidings of the breakfast-table. Batteries, soldiers, and generals were hurried hither and thither, stern investigations were ordered, guards doubled, and above it all rose the sound of popular comment in newspapers and on street corners, until the buzz spread through the nation. To be sure, the horse was not stolen, if we call the *Michigan* a horse, but there was an immense amount of shutting the stable door. And when the old steed appeared again in the various harbors of the lake, she was regarded with curiosity and redoubled affection as one who had indeed snuffed the battle, though from afar.

In less than four months Beall was captured near the Suspension-Bridge, and taken to New York. An attempt to bribe the turnkey with three thousand dollars in gold having been discovered, the authorities sent him to Fort Lafayette, and while there he made an appeal to the bar of New York to undertake his defense. For a time no one responded, but at length Mr. James T. Brady offered his services, and the trial began before a military court. Beall was charged with the seizure of the steamer *Philo Parsons* at Kelley's Island, Lake Erie; with the seizure of the steamer *Island Queen* at Middle Bass Island, Lake Erie; with being a rebel spy in Ohio and New York; and with an attempt to throw the express car off the track between Buffalo and Dunkirk, for the purpose of robbing the express company's safe. The officers of the captured steamers came from the West to identify him, and it is said that Beall frankly confirmed their testimony, remarking that as regarded the lake affair the trial had been fair and impartial. In the defense a manifesto from Jefferson Davis was offered, asserting that these acts upon the border were committed by his authority, and should be recognized as the acts of lawful belligerents. But the court pronounced the verdict of "Guilty;" and General Dix approved the finding, ordering the prisoner to be hung on Governor's Island, Saturday, the 18th of February. In reviewing the testimony, General Dix said: "The accused is shown to be a man of education and refinement, and it is difficult to account for his agency in transactions so abhorrent to the moral sense and so inconsistent with all the rules of honorable warfare." In this opinion all just-minded persons will agree. And yet, as an example of judgment, mistaken but equally sincere, an example of perverted mental vision, take the farewell letter of Beall to his brother, written on the eve of the day appointed for his execution:

"....Remember me kindly to my friends. Say to them that *I am not aware of committing any crime against society*. I die for my country. No thirst for blood or lucre animated me in my course....My hands

PUT-IN-BAY SCENERY.

are clean of blood, unless spilled in conflict, and not a cent enriched my pocket....Vengeance is mine, saith the Lord, and I will repay. Therefore do not show unkindness to the prisoners; they are helpless.

"JOHN YATES BEALL."

A short respite was afterward granted by President Lincoln to enable the mother to see her son; but on the afternoon of the 24th of February the execution took place, upon Governor's Island, New York Harbor, the prisoner responding to the prayers of the Episcopal service for the dying, but otherwise remaining apparently unmoved. One item in the newspaper accounts of the day is worthy of note. During the whole of the long proceedings before the execution the young man kept his eyes steadfastly fixed upon the southern horizon, as if looking toward the very heart of the country for which he was giving up his life.

Beall was finely formed, about five feet eight inches in height, with hazel eyes, brown hair and beard, and a firmly compressed mouth. He was thirty-two years old at the time of his death.

The islands are now free from alarm, the prison barracks on Johnson's, in the bay, are gone, and nothing warlike remains save a few earth-works and traditions of the past, which mingle the stories of 1813 with those of 1864. Grapes are every where: the long ranks of the vines stretch from shore to shore, and even the talk is fruity. Grapes are fastidious in their choice of a home;

here they will and there they will not grow. One side of a field they accept, and the other side they reject, and in many localities they refuse to show even a leaf on the trellis. If the soil is unfavorable for the vine, no art can render it favorable. But here on this southern shore of Lake Erie, and upon its islands, the grape flourishes in unrivaled luxuriance, and even the banks of the Ohio, the first stronghold of the Catawba, have been forced to yield a precedence in many points to the northern rival. Many crops are useful, but few are in themselves beautiful; digging potatoes, for example, can never figure upon the poet's page. But every thing connected with a vineyard is full of beauty, whether it be the green leaves and twining tendrils of the spring, the bunches slowly turning in the hot midsummer sun, the first picking in early fall, when the long aisles are filled with young girls making merry over their work, or the last ingathering of the Indian summer, when the late-ripening bunches hanging on the bare trellises shine through the vineyards in red-purple gleams as far as the eye can reach. Nothing can be more lovely than the islands in this golden season; Dionysius himself would have loved them. The water is blue and tranquil, for even in a gale the fury does not enter here among the landlocked harbors; on all sides stand the islets, some large, some small, some vine-covered and inhabited, others rocky and wild;

ON PUT-IN-BAY ISLAND.

the trees glow with color, and sweeping down to the water's edge, send a brilliant reflection far out from shore; and over all is spread the dreamy haze of Indian summer, more beautiful when resting on the water, and deepening here and there upon an island, than it ever can be on the level main-land. A few sail are seen, generally the fishing boats, but sometimes comes a Lake Erie yacht from the shore cities, bound to or from the duck marshes far up Sandusky Bay.

Gibraltar Island, a mere dot in the water, is crowned by a villa whose tower forms a picturesque point in the landscape. This islet is a country-seat belonging to Mr. Jay Cooke, the banker, and upon its rocky summit is a memorial of Commodore Perry, overlooking the scene of the battle of Lake Erie. Upon Kelley's Island also there are some handsome residences, and no doubt they will be built all through the archipelago whereever a point or a headland can be spared from the grapes. "Oh," said our oarsman, as we floated near the Needle's Eye of Gibraltar, "my brother-in-law could have bought the whole island for seventy-five dollars!"

"Why did he not do it, then?"

"Oh, he never thought as how the old rock would be worth so much; that was before folks took to coming here, and there wasn't many grapes either."

Thousands of dollars are now asked for the smallest island.

Kelley's, the largest of the group, possesses, in addition to its vineyards, valuable limestone quarries, from which the furnaces from Erie, Pennsylvania, to Marquette, Lake Superior, draw their supplies of lime and flux stone. It has 836 inhabitants, five schools, and four churches.

Put-in-Bay Island has 600 inhabitants, and two large hotels, which are filled in the summer with Southerners fleeing from Missouri and Kentucky heat; they find Lake Erie air quite cool, while the Lake Erie people, panting and oppressed, fly by on steamers, and stop not until they reach Mackinac or Lake Superior. Meanwhile the Lake Superior people make excursions to the north shore; and no doubt when the north shore is settled, the inhabitants will spend their summers at the arctic circle. The scenery of the islands is never grand, but always lovely. The tired brain is not excited to the work of admiration or wonder, but it can find restful pleasure floating on the quiet water in the shade of the cliffs, or dreaming away the days in the beautiful vineyards. We all have our moods when we ask, like the lotos-eaters,

"Why are we weighed upon with heaviness,
  And utterly consumed with sharp distress,
  While all things else have rest from weariness?"

At such times the islands are like the "land in which it seemed always afternoon," and coming here, the weary can fall "asleep in a half dream," and take sweet rest after their labors in the busy main-land towns.

America has so long imported its wines that it hardly yet realizes the presence of a native production. The wine of the islands is of several kinds, the best known being the dry Catawba. The expression "juice of the grape," however, misleads the ignorant, who fancy that grapes and a press are all that is necessary. This idea is like that of the young lady who, upon being asked how she would prepare a dish of baked beans, replied, "Why, put them in the dish and bake them, of course." Every thing has its chemistry, even beans; and wine-making is chemical science, whereof the very terms are mysterious to the uninitiated. But the grapes in the heaped barrels and baskets are a sight worth seeing, and the presses, with the juice flowing out in a fragrant stream, bring the Old Testament to our minds, the days when the new wine was preferred to the old. Down in the cellars of the wine-houses, under the presses, stand rows of giant casks, and the superintendent fills a glass from each to show the wine in all its stages. It is good—very good; and as it is native, it is cheap—cheap when compared with even the poorest imported mixture. It has often been asserted that the inhabitants of a vine-growing district are never intemperate. The purity of the wine prevents the excitement produced by vile compounds, and its very plentifulness teaches its proper use. There is no need to slip away into obscure places to get it; there is no need for deception or excuse. Every body has it, every body drinks it, and the fascination of rarity is gone. If this is true, the native wines should be brought into common use as an antidote against the deadly liquors which so soon blunt the heart and destroy the mind of man. Throughout the West already have they won their way, and gradually are they penetrating into the Eastern markets. Not rapidly, however, for it was only last summer when, after ordering a bottle of dry Catawba, which by some chance had got its name upon the wine list of a fashionable watering-place hotel, the head waiter brought us "sparkling Moselle," with the assurance that it was "just the same wine—exactly the same." The statistics of the grapes and wine for one year will give an idea of the extent of the production:

Number of acres in bearing in Ottowa County
    and the islands........................ 2,032
Total product, in pounds 7,462,750
Grapes sold, in pounds 118,000
Number of gallons of wine made.......... 312,134

The grapes bring from five to eight cents per pound, and the common quality of wine at wholesale brings sixty cents per gallon.

There are good years and bad years, the vintage varying in quality and quantity. Already the wine of such-and-such a year is offered to the guest with an air which would be foreign if it was not so entirely native; old-fashioned connoisseurs know all about the vintage of such and such a year, but in their day the vintages spoken of were all foreign.

They are not all foreign now. The native Bacchus is young and modest, but his followers will gather around him before long. Already the native poet, America's greatest, has not been ashamed to chant his praises in the following verses:

OTHER TITLES IN THE "OLD/100 YEARS AGO" SERIES:

GEORGIA 100 YEARS AGO
Includes: The City of Atlanta; The City of Savannah; and A Georgia Corn-Shucking. Contains 35 Illustrations.

LOUISIANA 100 YEARS AGO — VOL. I
Includes: Old and New Louisiana. Contains 37 Illustrations.

LOUISIANA 100 YEARS AGO — VOL. II
Includes: Old and New Louisiana. Contains 33 Illustrations.

TEXAS 100 YEARS AGO
Includes: Through Texas, and San Antonio De Bexar. Contains 35 Illustrations.

COLORADO 100 YEARS AGO
Includes: The Metropolis of the Rocky Mountains; The City of Denver; and the Wheeler Expedition in Southern Colorado. Also contains 30 Illustrations.

NORTHERN CALIFORNIA 100 YEARS AGO
Includes: San Francisco; The Sacramento Valley; Mendocino and Clear Lake; and Mount Shasta. Contains 20 Illustrations.

SOUTHERN CALIFORNIA 100 YEARS AGO — VOL. I
Includes: Southern California, Parts 1 & 2, and The Lick Observatory of California. Contains 27 Illustrations.

SOUTHERN CALIFORNIA 100 YEARS AGO — VOL. II
Includes: Southern California, Part 3, and A Santa Barbara Holiday. Also contains 31 Illustrations.

HAWAII-NEI, THE KINGDOM OF HAWAII, 100 YEARS AGO
Contains 47 Illustrations.

CHRISTMAS 100 YEARS AGO
Includes: Christmas; Christmas Throughout Christendom; and The Voice of Christmas Past. Also contains 37 Illustrations.

Price of each book is $3.50 plus $.50 Postage and Handling. Available from Sun Publishing Co., P.O. Box 4383, Albuquerque, New Mexico 87106, U.S.A.

A DAY AMONG THE QUAKERS IN CENTRAL OHIO

BY MRS. NELLIE EYSTER

ALONG a portion of Lake Erie's southern shore, where an enchanting variety of cedar groves, rocky bluffs, a shell-dotted beach, and houses rich in architectural beauty offer a long succession of enjoyment to both the heart and eyes of a tourist, there rises above all else a land light-house, founded upon a rock and built of purest granite. Near by, it looks a tower of strength; afar off, it seems like a huge white finger pointing upward; yet, near or far, it stands out from amidst all surroundings with a distinctness, or an individuality, that makes it a nucleus around which all other associations of the shore scenery gather. The following, in bold relief, from the adventures of a few weeks' summer wandering, is a single episode, *whose details I give with careful truthfulness:*

The time was July, 1868; the day, a Sabbath; and the place, an out-of-the-way settlement in Central Ohio.

Grace Newton, whom Ruth Clifford and I were visiting, had told us of a little colony of Quakers, not very far off—anti-progressive ones—who held on tenaciously to the faith of their fathers, and had no companionship with the villagers who worshiped once a month in the Methodist chapel, "down the road;" and when she proposed to have Dick harnessed in the spring wagon, and drive us to Oakhill Meeting-house, four miles distant, we offered no opposition. The wagon had no top. The sun's rays were almost scorching. A portable seat, in the middle of the wagon, accommodated Ruth and me, under shelter of an umbrella, while Grace, in her character of Jehu, occupied a low-backed chair in front.

That ride was guiltless of any monotony. Bouncing, jolting, half shaken to pieces, now down in a rut, then heaved over a stump, now plashing through a stream which ran across the road, then rolling through a foot in depth of soft clay, down a steep hill, with a cry from Grace, "Hold my chair, girls, or I'll slide out!" Thence up one, with another call, "Push me front, girls, or I'll slide back!" And every few minutes, as the low-hanging tree boughs brushed against us, dodging our heads to escape the fate of Absalom, we might well be thankful when the last long graveled hill was ascended, and the low, weather-beaten, board meeting-house stood before us. Its surroundings reminded me of a Southern camp-meeting; for every tree near by sheltered a carriage of some kind, while a corral of horses switched off flies in a long shed, built for their accommodation.

"How long has meeting set, boys?" asked Grace of two little urchins, who were slyly creeping around a rock with their Sunday hats full of dead-ripe blackberries.

"Jes half 'n hour," said one.

"Then we will disturb the preacher," said Ruth.

"Blissful ignorance!" exclaimed Grace. "It is easy to see you were never in a Quaker meeting. Follow me, doing just as I do."

The interior of the building was separated in half by a partition containing numerous holes a foot square, which divided the sexes. The pews were elevated like those in a theatre, the very young people being packed near the ceiling, and the elders occupying those nearest the floor. It may seem strange that Ruth and I had never seen Quakers at worship; but this was really our first opportunity; nor had we any but the crudest idea of their formula. Nothing human could have looked more sanctimonious than the brethren and sisters, each with folded hands and downcast eyes, as they sat in a silence so profound I grew nervous with hearing my own heart beat.

"For what are they waiting, Grace? I can not endure this another quarter of an hour," I said.

"Oh, do be still!" she replied, in the faintest of whispers. "They are waiting on the Spirit; it will soon move some one, I hope."

Waiting on the Spirit! Why, its presence was visible to me wherever I looked through the opened door. A voice from out the ripening grain seemed crying, "Lo! 'tis here." The birds that soared toward the sun half warbled, "There, up there." The soft wind caught the sweet refrain, and murmured, "Every where." Only man was silent.

The church took its name from a gigantic oak which stood just in front of the door, stretching out its "hundred arms so strong" so near at some points that the leaves lay against the whitewashed boards. Its trunk was hollow, and an old ram, panting from the excessive heat, had thrust his head and shoulders in it for relief in the cool darkness. I studied the hind-quarters of this venerable mutton until I had counted every knot upon its woolly back; then, by way of diversion, again sought the faces of the elderly sisterhood. Than some few, nothing in the ripe maturity of modest womanhood was lovelier. With downcast eyes, hands folded quietly in their laps, and scarcely any perceptible heavings of the motherly bosoms beneath their spotlessly white neckerchiefs, they looked, each one, an impersonation of that peace which "passeth understanding;" but statues were scarcely quieter. Presently I espied a middle-aged man, whose broad brim covered his eyebrows, move his hands once or twice, as though washing them in an invisible basin; then he crossed and uncrossed his feet, sighed heavily three times with inspiration deep enough to fill the lungs of a blacksmith's bellows, finally rose, opened his mouth, and spoke. Written words can not describe his nasal intonations, nor the peculiar inflections of his unpleasant voice. His theme was the uselessness of mere learning as a means of spiritual advancement— and his abuse of the rules of rhetoric and grammar the strongest argument in proof of the sincerity of his belief. How he sweated as his excitement increased! How he sawed the air with his long arms, and see-sawed from heel-tip to toe! "Yes, my brethren—ah—and you, my sisters—ah—labor not for the meat which perishes—ah—take no scrip in your hand—ah—nor money in your purse—ah (ironically speaking—ah)—and then may be, like St. Paul—ah—you'll be gifted with an un—n—n—n—atural eloquence."

Such was the peroration of his half hour's discourse, when he resumed his seat under a silence which would have been most flattering to the orator of any but a Quaker meeting. Whose voice would be the next to arouse the attention of that waiting and undemonstrative audience? The query was answered by the old ram, who, walking straight up to the front-door, put his head in it, made a brief but deliberate survey of the congregation, and then, uttering a loud, prolonged baa-a, returned to the shelter of the oak. Oh, the laughs that were choked back, and the rosy lips that were bitten into a deeper carmine the few next minutes! But the elder who had spoken suddenly ended the restraint by shaking hands with the neighbor next him, which was the signal for the universal hand-shaking that closes every meeting. It may have been an outside show—I know not; but the show, as such, was the most suggestive of that Christian fellowship which should unite those who cherish the same faith I ever saw.

"How is thee, Grace Norton?"

The voice was that of the elder who had spoken in the meeting.

"I am well. This is my friend Ruth Clifford, Nathaniel Grubb, of whose coming I told thee. How is Aunt Betsey?"

"She took cold last Lord's-day when it rained on us. If this was not another Lord's-day, I would like to tell thee what she says about that honey thee is wanting to buy. Thee can have six pounds of it at forty cents a pound, and that is dead cheap."

"Ah, Friend Grubb!" I thought, "'ye pay tithe of mint and anise and cummin, and have omitted the weightier matters of the law.'" I turned to watch the approach of a fair old lady in drab silk bonnet and spectacles, who was nearing us with a face radiant in kindness. Ruth, who also saw her, with her usual impulsiveness, sprang forward and grasped her extended hand.

"Are you not Aunt Phœbe Haddam?" she said. "You must excuse my boldness, but my friend Grace Norton has written to me so often of your kindness to her, when she was sick and a stranger, I felt I would know you if I ever saw your face."

"Thee is right. That is my name; but thee overrates a simple act of duty, my child."

They were acquainted already, which resulted in an invitation to us three to come home and dine with her, adding, "I know father will be glad to converse with thee."

Grace and Ruth eagerly accepted it, allowing me, at my request, to return to Snowden with a Quaker family and be entertained by little Gay, the daughter of Grace.

What Ruth saw and heard, and what I missed in not sharing her eventful visit, I will tell as it was told to me. Grace and she followed in the spring wagon close behind the barouche which contained Aunt Phœbe, her daughter Rebecca, and son Simon, who was driving. The distance was two miles, through a long strip of woodland and most delicious shade.

"These Haddams are the most interesting Quakers I know," said Grace; "but the folks around here think Uncle Samuel, the husband, a little queer, and not quite sound of mind. He rarely goes from home now, having a disease in his eyes which makes him almost blind—but you must not allow me to prejudice you against him, for his character is irreproachable. Indeed, I know very little of him but from hearsay."

This explanation, kindly as it was given, dampened Ruth's ardor, and made her rather shrink from the visit now so near. They entered a lane, and soon reined up before a small white cottage, whose yard was encircled by a thick hedge of Osage orange. Not another house was any where visible. The spot could scarcely have been more isolated had it been in the centre of the Great Sahara, but there the resemblance ended, for whatever of beauty there is in undulating hills covered with verdure, patches of woods, running water, and browsing kine, were there in profusion.

"Don't wait here in the sun, Ruth; just follow the path to the house," said Aunt Phœbe.

Grace stopped to help Simon tie up "old Dick," and Ruth walked on up an avenue of blooming hollyhocks to where a door stood wide open. How white was the sanded sill, and how neat the home-made rug which lay just at the entrance! Seeing no one, she stepped in, when suddenly from an arm-chair there arose a tall, slender old man, who confronted her. His appearance was remarkable. His dress was of fine white linen, without spot or color, except that of the narrow black ribbon knotted under his broad, unstarched shirt-collar. His thin hair was white and fine as spun glass, and his face—the skin of which was fair as a girl's—of most benignant and intellectual expression. His eyes alone were not visible, being protected by large green goggles. Ruth stood an instant motionless. Such a vision of majestic old age, in such a place, she had never dreamed of seeing.

"Thy footsteps are those of a stranger. Enter. Thou art welcome," was his salutation.

Ruth advanced, laying her hand in his large, soft palm, with a few simple words of greeting.

"Thy hand is that of a gentlewoman, and thy voice is low and pleasant. Who art thou?" said he.

"My name is Ruth Clifford. I have come from the capital of Pennsylvania to visit my friend Grace Norton. I accompanied her to meeting this morning, and was invited home to dinner by Aunt Phœbe Haddam."

"Thou hast come, then, from the great world of which I know so little. God—ever blessed be His holy name—has seen fit to take away my sight; but I have witnessed the coming of the Lord, and mine eyes have seen the salvation of His people, so I am content," and clasping his hands, his lips moved as if in prayer.

Ruth's emotions were those of awe, reverence, and admiration commingled. She recalled Grace's language, that Uncle Samuel—for of course this was he—was "a little queer," and wondered whether he might not only be that, to some minds, incomprehensible thing—a religious enthusiast. His articulation was very distinct, every word having a purity of finish which would have been marked in the diction of a professed elocutionist. How much more astonishing, then, from the lips of this unassuming, humble Quaker farmer, who had doubtless never been beyond the limits of his native State.

Before he again spoke, his old wife, with her daughter and Grace, came in.

"Now, dear, thee must feel at home," said Aunt Phœbe, taking Ruth's hat. "We are plain people; but thee and Grace are truly welcome. Has thee felt lonely this morning, father?" she asked, pushing aside a stray lock of his silvery hair with which a breeze was toying. "Did thy poor eyes pain thee much?"

His smile was perfect, as he replied:

"Oh no, mother; I forgot my eyes. *His* words came to me very clear: 'For our light affliction, which is but for a moment, worketh for us a far more exceeding and eternal weight of glory; while we look not at the things which are seen, but at the things which are not seen; for the things which are seen are temporal; but the things which are not seen are eternal.' I thank thee for bringing the young woman home. I will enjoy her speech."

"I am the one to feel grateful, Sir. May I call you Uncle Samuel?"

"Yes, if it pleaseth thee."

"Well, Uncle Samuel, I have traveled over several thousand miles since I left home, but never before got into a place like this. Every thing charms me, and I am glad of the privilege to just sit still and hear you talk."

"Hush, hush! Thou must not flatter!" Yet the old man's tones expressed pleasure withal, for Ruth's were full of earnestness.

Aunt Phœbe's kind heart was gratified.

"I see thee can entertain each other," she said, "so I will get the dinner."

Rebekah and Grace went to assist her, and Ruth and the old man were left alone.

He broke the silence first, saying:

"Hast thou seen General Grant, and dost thou think him a good man? I have longed to hear his voice, and daily pray to God that he will strengthen his hands, and make him worthy of the great work to which he is called."

Ruth said she knew him only through his works, but felt that he, perhaps more than any living American, would perfect the grand schemes left unfinished by the death of Lincoln.

At that name the old man's face lighted up with a beauty almost angelic. Turning toward Ruth, who sat near his chair, and laying his hand lightly on hers, he said, eagerly:

"Hast thou seen Mr. Lincoln?"

"Yes, Sir," replied Ruth. "Once, when living, I stood so near him that every line of his face was as visible to me as yours now. It was the last time he ever addressed an audience as Abraham Lincoln, the citizen; for a few days afterward he was inaugurated President of these United States. Once again I stood very near him; but it was to look upon his coffined form lying in state in our Capitol. Did *you* ever see him?"

"Ah! yes, yes; and a sadder face than his was *then* I never looked upon."

Ruth's face was luminant with curiosity.

"Why, Uncle Samuel! Where was he? What were the circumstances? Do tell me!"

"Perhaps thou wilt not sympathize with me. I rarely speak of these things save among my own people. In what light dost thou view the colored race?"

Now the freeing of the slaves and the education of the freedmen had long been among Ruth's hobbies; so when called upon to "rehearse the articles of her belief," she did it so promptly and forcibly that no one could doubt her philanthropy nor ardent desire for justice to that long-suffering and terribly wronged people.

Uncle Samuel was now in his element. Cut off by old age, blindness, and his isolated home from the busy world, only echoes of the mighty questions which were agitating the greatest minds of our country had reached him; and to have unexpectedly a companion, young, full of ardor and enthusiasm, dropping down, as it were, upon his very hearth-stone, was a pleasure such as rarely occurred in his quiet life.

"Now tell me, Uncle Samuel. When and where did *you* meet Mr. Lincoln?"

"I scarcely ever speak of it now, my child," he said, folding his thin hands, his face becoming sweetly grave and his words falling very slowly.

"My quiet life has known few storms. I have loved God as my first, best, and dearest friend, and he has ever dealt most tenderly with me. I always abhorred slavery. During the first years of the great rebellion, when I read and heard what was the condition of the poor enslaved negroes, I tried to think it was a cunning device of bad men to create greater enmity between the North and South; but when I read Mr. Lincoln's speeches I thought so good a man as I believed him to be could not lie, and then I resolved to go and see for myself. At one of our First-day meetings I spoke my intention to the brethren, but although feeling as I did upon the subject, they said it was rash for me to expose my life, for I could do no good by such means. Nevertheless I went, traveling on horseback through most of the Southern States. My life was often in great danger, but there was an invisible arm ever between me and the actual foe, and after some weeks I returned, saying the half had not been told me of the sufferings of those poor, *poor*, despised, yet God-trusting and God-fearing, people."

Here his voice expressed a fullness of pity which could come from no source but the depths of a loving and large heart.

"That summer (it was in '62) I plowed and reaped and gathered in my little harvest as usual. Day by day I prayed at home and in the field that God would show his delivering power as he had to the children of Israel; but nothing seemed to come in answer.

"Now and then, during the beginning of the war, news reached us of a battle having been fought by our men, and a victory gained, but still the poor colored people were not let go. Then one night I had a singular dream, and I said, 'Yea, Lord! thy servant heareth.' I soon made ready and said to mother:

"'Wilt thou go with me to Washington to see the President?'

"'Where thou goest, I will go,' she answered.

"My good friends called me insane. Some said this trip was even more foolish than the last; that I knew no one in Washington, and would never gain access to the great President.

"The good Lord knew I did not mean to be fool-hardy, but I had that on my mind which I was to tell him, and I had faith to believe that He who feeds the sparrows would watch over me.

"Art thou tired, child?"

"No, no, Sir. Please go on."

"We left here on a pleasant September morning—the first time that mother had been from home thirty miles in fifty years, and now hundreds lay before us. Before we went out of the door we prayed that God would guide our wanderings, or, if He saw best, direct us back again. Every one looked at and spoke to us kindly on our journey from near Cincinnati to Harrisburg, and, when we got out there to change cars and rest a while, we felt that so far the Lord had prospered us. It was remarkable that a man who was at the dépôt (and a pleasant manner he had, too) said:

"'Friend, do you stop here?'

"I answered, 'Yes. We are weary, and will rest to-night.'

"'Come home with me, then,' he said. 'My wife was born a Quaker, and will be glad to entertain you.'

"We went. His home was beautiful. The Lord had abundantly blessed him, and that night I was calm and happy. We got to Washington the next evening. It was early candle-light, and there was so much confusion mother clung to my arm, exclaiming:

"'Oh, Samuel, we ought not to have come here. It is like Babel.'

"'Have faith, mother,' I said. 'The Lord will send help if we are doing right;' and we walked away from the cars.

"Under a gas-post a man was standing, reading a small letter. I stepped before him and said:

"'Good friend, wilt thou tell us where to find President Lincoln?'

"He looked us all over before he spoke. We were neat and clean. Soon his face got bright and smiling, and he asked us a few plain questions. I told him we were Friends from Ohio, who had come all these miles to say a few words to Mr. Lincoln.

"He bade us come with him, and, taking us to a great house called Willard's Hotel, put us in a little room away off from the noise.

"'Stay here,' said he, 'and I will see when the President can admit you.'

"He staid a long time. Meanwhile a young man brought us a nice supper, which was very kind and thoughtful in him, and when the gentleman came back he handed me a slip of paper which read: 'Admit the bearer to the chamber of the President at nine o'clock to-morrow morning.'

"My heart was so full of gratitude I could not speak my thankfulness. That night was as peaceful as those in our little home in the meadow.

"The next morning the kind gentleman came and conducted us to the house in which the President was. Every body whom we met seemed to know our new friend, and touched their hats to him. I was glad so many people seemed to like him. At the door he left us, promising to return in an hour. The room in which we were now shown was full of persons, all waiting to see Mr. Lincoln. Mother said, 'Ah, Samuel! we will not get near him to-day. See these anxious faces who came before us.'

"'As God wills,' said I.

"It was a sad place we were in. There were soldiers' wives and mothers sitting about, and not a soul from which joy and pleasure did not seem to have fled. Some were even weeping, and I thought what a fearfully solemn thing it was to hold much power. They found in some way that I would soon see the President; then how they begged me to intercede for them with him! One poor mother whose only boy was dying with home-sickness—" here Uncle Samuel's voice got husky with the sad memory, and tears fell from his sightless eyes upon his withered hands.

Ruth reverently brushed them off, and in a few minutes he proceeded:

"When the summons came for us to enter (it was in advance of the rest) my knees smote together, and for an instant I tottered. 'Keep heart, Samuel,' said mother, and we went forward. I fear thou wilt think me vain if I tell what followed."

"No fear, Sir. Please proceed."

"It seemed so wonderful; for a minute I could not realize that such humble people as we were should be there in the actual presence of the greatest man in the world. Then he received us so kindly. I can not express his manner. He shook hands with us, and placed his chair between us. Oh, how I honored the good man! But I said:

"'Mr. Lincoln, wilt thou pardon me that I do not remove my hat?' He smiled, and his face all lit up as he replied:

"'Certainly; I understand about it.'

"The dear, *dear* man," and again Uncle Samuel stopped, as though to revel in the memory of that interview.

"What then, Sir?" Ruth was impatient.

The answer came with a solemnity indescribable.

"*Of that half-hour's conversation it does not become me to speak; I will think of it through eternity.* At last we had to go. He took a hand of each of us in his, and said, looking straight in our eyes, 'Father, mother, I thank you for this visit; God bless you!'

"Was there ever greater condescension than that? At the last moment I asked him if he would object to just writing a line, certifying that we had fulfilled our mission, so we could show it in council. He sat down at his table—Wilt thou open the upper drawer of that old secretary and hand me a little tin box therein?"

Ruth obeyed, placing in his now trembling fingers a small square box, bright as silver. Taking from it a folded paper he bade Ruth read. The words were *literally* as follows:

"I take pleasure in asserting that I have had a pleasant and profitable intercourse with Friend Samuel Haddam and his wife, Phœbe Haddam. May the Lord comfort them as they have comforted me.
"ABRAHAM LINCOLN.
"*September* 20, 1862."

"Oh, Uncle Samuel!" exclaimed Ruth. "I can scarcely realize it, that I should, away out here in this *almost* backwoods, read words traced by our beloved Mr. Lincoln's own hands. How very singular!"

"Not more than the whole event was to us, dear child, from first to last. The following Monday, the preliminary Proclamation of Emancipation was issued. Thank God! Thank God!"

It is impossible to depict the devout fervor of the old patriarch's thanksgiving.

"We found our friend," he continued, "waiting for us. When we showed him the testimonial, he nodded his head in affirmation, and said,

"It is well."

"We soon left Washington, for our work was done, and I was satisfied *now* to go home again. Our good friend escorted us to the omnibus which took us to the cars, having treated us throughout with a hospitality I can never forget. May God care for him as he did for us."

"Did you learn his name, Sir?"

"He is high in the estimation of men, and his name is Salmon P. Chase."

The dinner in that peaceful Quaker house was like all else about it—real and informal. Simon proved himself worthy of his noble parentage, and Rebecca, who was engaged in teaching a Freedman's school, some miles from home, was as companionable as earnest in her philanthropic work. Uncle Samuel was happy. He had revived once more *the event* of his life, and electric currents of an awakened vitality were flashing through his sluggish veins. He sought to amuse Ruth, by having Simon open a cupboard and place in her hands, one by one, curious fossils, shells, minerals, and other articles of *vertu*, the gleanings of his leisure hours. His knowledge of geology was astonishing, and in each mineral he read a record of God's unerring wisdom.

But evening was approaching, and old Dick having been reharnessed, the parting from so much that was endearing had to come. Ruth felt it was no mere hand-shake of courtesy which grasped her so firmly, when Aunt Phœbe, in her motherly way, thanked her for the pleasure their visit had afforded them. The last "good-by" was for Uncle Samuel. As Ruth approached the venerable saint he arose.

"My child! I thank thee for thy sympathy, which will ever be to me a sweet memory. We will not meet again here; I am very near home, and only wait my Father's summons. Live near to Christ. There alone is the Way, the Truth, and the Life." Then laying his hand upon her head, he added: "The Lord bless thee and keep thee; The Lord make His face to shine upon thee and be gracious to thee: The Lord lift up His countenance upon thee and give thee peace forever. Amen." And stooping, he kissed her forehead.

"I can not possibly describe to you the grand simplicity of that pure old man," added Ruth, when her recital was ended. "I have quoted our conversation, word for word; but could no more give you his pathetic tones than I could arrange in bars and notes the song of a lark. God alone knows to what extent Mr. Lincoln was influenced by that half-hour's conversation to the performance of that great deed which set a nation free; but I can not help feeling I have read a page in that wonderful man's history which would have been sealed to me but for my unexpected meeting with that precious old Quaker."